Art Therapy in a Children's Community

ART THERAPY
IN A
CHILDREN'S COMMUNITY

*A Study of the Function of Art Therapy
in the Treatment Program of
Wiltwyck School for Boys*

EDITH KRAMER

With a Foreword by
VIOLA W. BERNARD, M.D.

SCHOCKEN BOOKS · NEW YORK

First published by SCHOCKEN BOOKS 1977

Copyright 1958, by Edith Kramer

Library of Congress Cataloging in Publication Data

Kramer, Edith.
 Art therapy in a children's community.

 Reprint of the ed. published by Thomas, Springfield, Ill., which was issued as no. 318 in American lecture series.
 Bibliography: p. 227
 Includes index.
 1. Art therapy. 2. Child psychotherapy—Residential treatment. 3. Wiltwyck School for Boys, Esopus, N.Y.
 I. Title.

[RJ505.A7K72 1977]   618.9′28′915   77-75292

Manufactured in the United States of America

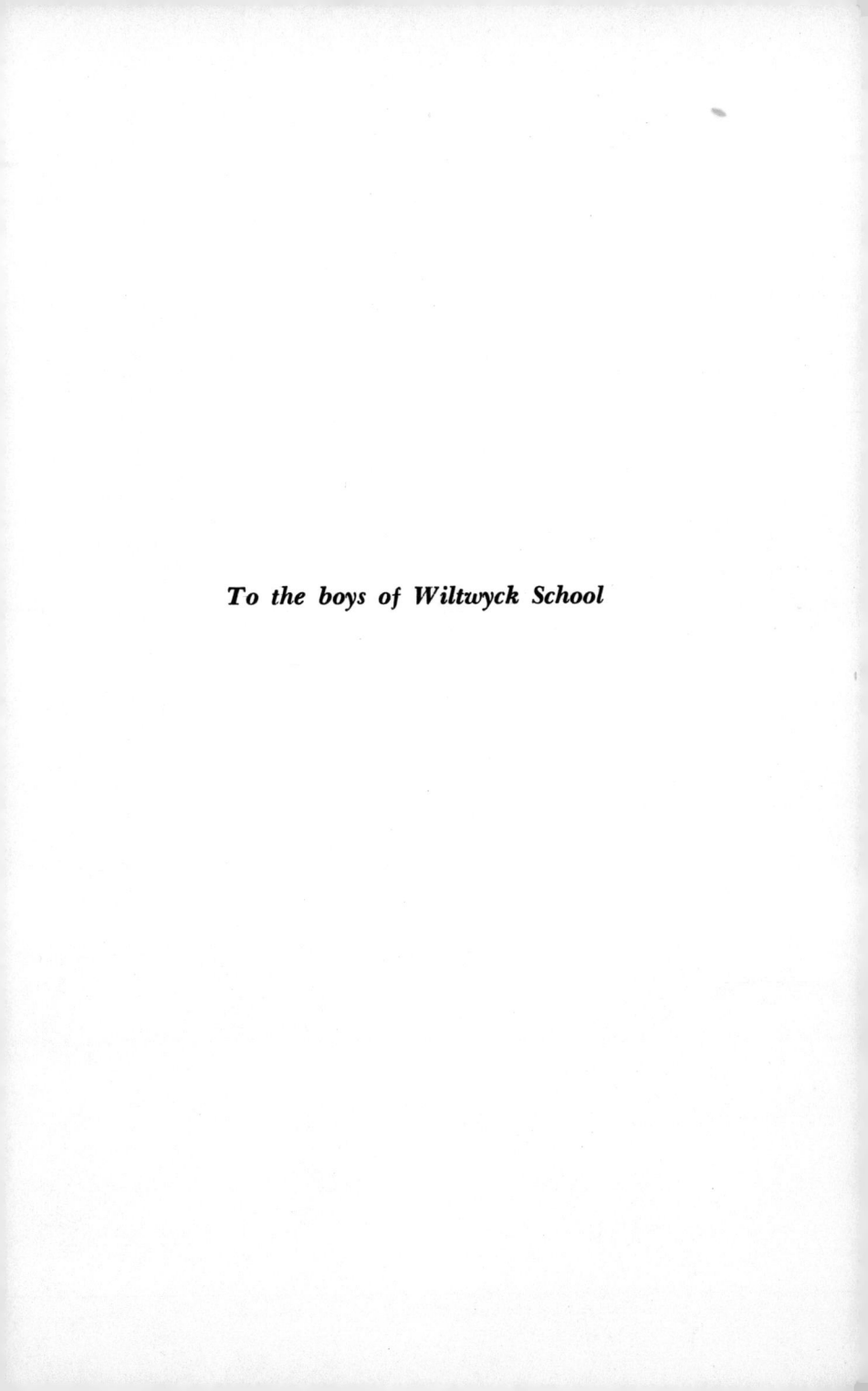

To the boys of Wiltwyck School

PREFACE

It gives me great pleasure to see this book made available to a larger public. Since it was written art therapy has gained much ground. When I began work at Wiltwyck School in 1950 the field was still untried. Except for Margaret Naumburg's pioneering work there was no literature to guide the novice. My seven years at Wiltwyck were formative ones for me. Even though ideas first formulated in response to the experience have been developed, broadened and modified in the course of time, I find myself adhering to the tenets I presented in this first attempt at understanding art as therapy. I regret that it was not possible to improve on the book's stylistic ineptitudes. Most grating among them is the self-conscious avoidance of the first personal pronoun. Today I should most certainly not write "the therapist" when I mean to speak of myself.

This generation's readers may find certain descriptions of black children's attitudes toward the color of their skin objectionable. Between 1950 and 1957 the word "black," now in common usage, still constituted an insult in the average Afro-American child's mind. The tragic self-denigration which made them reluctant to paint dark skin color was still much in evidence. Martin's story, pages 60–65, exemplifies the fundamental change in the black community's attitude toward its African heritage. The events occurred in 1950–52, even before the 1954 Supreme Court decision. Martin's parents' pride in their African heritage was at the time unusual among American blacks. They were ahead of their time and their son had to suffer for their pride.

Throughout the book references to racial problems might seem dated, or worse, arouse anger. Yet these descriptions truthfully present the racial climate of the fifties.

The eminent receptiveness to the arts among boys such as those who painted at Wiltwyck School persists unchanged. The need for art therapy programs for them is as urgent today as it was in 1958.

EDITH KRAMER

1977

INTRODUCTION

Art Therapy, as evolved by Edith Kramer, engages the creative process, through painting, towards the goals of overall personality growth and rehabilitation. In presenting this remarkably original and lucid interpretive account of Art Therapy in a community of emotionally disturbed boys, the author through her rare facility with verbal as well as visual media, has herself accomplished a highly creative communication which actively involves the reader in moving and vivid experience.

I would expect this book to appeal to a wide range of readers beyond those immediately concerned with Art Therapy because of the breadth as well as depth of Miss Kramer's approach. Throughout her exposition she moves freely from the theoretical to the practical and back again, livening and documenting her generalizations with case material, and deriving general principles from specific clinical evidence. She keeps in view both the larger social perspectives and the individual minutiae of the complex processes—artistic, educational, developmental, intrapsychic and interpersonal—of which Art Therapy is a composite.

Art Therapy, as developed by Edith Kramer, differs in some respects from other reported Art Therapy programs. The broad basis of Kramer's program has been one of its distinctive features; she has worked with the total population of the same children's community over a period of years. (The Wiltwyck School for Boys will be familiar to some readers who may recall it as the setting of the film, *The Quiet One*.) This has enabled her to observe and influence many facets of interacting creative processes within the individual and the group; it has also made it possible for her to study and stimulate therapeutic movement in a boy over a protracted span in relation to other dynamic ingredients of his life at the institution and with respect to his family.

Thus, individual and group interplay is brilliantly illustrated by the described rise and decline of artistic fashions at Wiltwyck, such as the King, Prisoner and Monster periods of painting. Each series was originated by an artistically gifted child out of the linkage of his talent with his emotional conflicts, and was picked up and maintained insofar as it provided a form through which, with individual modifications, prevailing psychic needs and problems among group members could find expression and attempted solution. Psychodynamic correlations with these paintings and their differentiated diagnostic and therapeutic implications become unmistakably meaningful as we are shown, for instance, Jerry's nonchalant decorative prisoner, Walter's despairing overpowered prisoner, and Bernard's mutilated night-marish prisoner, as these are illuminated by Kramer's vignettes of each boy's personal history, personality patterns and the progression of his art therapy productions in the context of his overall adjustment and treatment at Wiltwyck.

Or to choose among many of the case examples of shorter or longer sequences of Art Therapy during a boy's stay at Wiltwyck, it is an impressive adventure in empathy to follow the ups and downs of nine-year old Frank's struggles for growth and to get on friendlier terms with himself and his world, through his Art Therapy experiences over an almost three year period. The dramatic contrast between Frank's early painting of the rigid powerful Indian Chief as an ambivalent security

Introduction xi

symbol and his painting of the Mexican, two years later, which "contains and expresses emotional content on a high level of sublimation", demonstrates with convincing impact Frank's developmental movement and gain of integrative capacity during the interval.

The author achieves unusual clarity of expression but without recourse to oversimplification or superficiality. Instead, this clarity reflects with what thorough assimilation she comprehends her very complex material. Original ideas are stated so simply that one feels one has always know them, and familiar concepts are put so freshly that they carry new impact of meaning. Miss Kramer's psychological insight, self-awareness, and consistent maintenance of her role as Art Therapist, has enabled her to master through understanding, and thus to bring into meaningful order material that might have overwhelmed a less well-equipped worker as a bombarding chaos of primitive and unconscious emotionality.

Indeed I felt in reading this book as though it were a distillate of a much greater quantity of ideas and observations that had been subjected to extensive refining and working through to its present highly concentrated form.

According to Miss Kramer, the art therapist must possess the specialized skills of artist, teacher and therapist all at once, and she finds occasions throughout the book to blend in how, when and why the art therapist should function. Theoretical explanations are offered for whatever practical methods she advocates, such as the theoretical usefulness of children's art folders and of a continuous exhibit of children's paintings in the dining room. On the other hand, her theorizing about the art therapist's roles and functioning is always concretized by specific examples, as with the therapeutic handling of a child's acting-out and "transference" relationship with the art therapist, for example. She is also refreshingly willing to cite her own mistakes in order that the reader, as well as she, can learn from them, as in the case of the "the big fist" episode.

Miss Kramer's understanding of the possibilities of Art Therapy for disturbed children of this age group (8-13 years) is fortunately coupled with her understanding of its limitations and her good judgment and sensitivity as to what not to do or say. It is clear that she wisely sees Art Therapy as one of several interdependent and mutually enhancing, rather than competing approaches to a troubled child. Thus with many of the children she works with she tells us of how this ties in for them with their psychotherapy, remedial reading, relationship with social worker or cottage counselor, etc.

Many of the emotionally deprived and disturbed children of the type who need Wiltwyck and other Wiltwycks are often discouragingly hard to treat by traditional clinical methods. Over-prone to the language of acting-out, they may not respond to solely verbal psychotherapy, nor dare to trust an adult psychotherapist or caseworker too soon in the frightening intimacy of a one-to-one treatment situation. Accustomed to school failures they may not risk further frustration and failure by accepting academic learning. Fearful, hostile, conflicted and immature they lack adequate resources for satisfying relationships with peers or adults and are the prey of their own primitive and unsocialized impulses. For such children the professional disciplines concerned are continuously seeking more effective ways of helping.

Much active debate is now current as to the best ways of planning in-patient facilities for emotionally disturbed children in terms of program, kinds of staff, etc. It seems to me that Miss Kramer's book has important applicability to some of these issues. Need for skillful, patient individualizing of these children, as she has enabled many of them to communicate so poignantly to us through her book, is a telling argument against planning treatment centers that rely solely on a humane milieu with schooling, activities and recreation, but essentially no individualized treatment based on psychodynamic understanding. On the other hand, Miss Kramer's kind of work seems to reach a number of these children who are unable or unready to profit from certain of the other methods, and to help some of them to get more out of the rest of the treatment program.

In essence, Miss Kramer's treatment takes advantage of the natural bent of latency and prepuberty children towards art, and of the special ways that painting can foster emotional maturation. Her work is firmly based on psychoanalytic psychology of which she has an unusually sound and subtle understanding. In very readable fashion, enhanced by the children's paintings, she explains how art bears a particular relation to the process of sublimation and can serve to bind and transform primitive aggression through a variety of the mental mechanisms. Through painting, these isolated joyless children may take first steps in satisfactory communication with their peers and overcome their habitual frustration and failure through a sense of mastery that can come from successful achievement and the acquisition of skill. Thus, children whose lives have lacked the necessary relationships and experience for healthy ego development are helped to overcome their deficiencies in maturation. Kramer beautifully describes the gradual steps towards ego consolidation of several of these children during the course of Art Therapy.

Throughout this book there radiates a therapeutic spirit of a high order. The author neither resorts to defeatism nor pressure for impossible treatment results in the face of these children's great handicaps and limitations, and yet can maintain her appreciation of each child's assets and potentialities, and her enthusiasm for helping him liberate and fulfill them. She has also been able to learn from the children so that she does indeed come to "touch upon the mystery of the structure and development of the artistic personality".

VIOLA W. BERNARD, M.D.

ACKNOWLEDGMENTS

I welcome this occasion to express my thanks to the staff of Wiltwyck School for Boys for their sustained cooperation and interest in the art therapy program. In particular, I am indebted to Mrs. Earline Hughley and Mr. Martin Hellman, social workers, and Mr. Herbert Nixon, head counselor, for their help in compiling the two long case histories of Part III. I also wish to thank the teachers and principals of P.S. 615 for their understanding and acceptance of the art therapy program which became part of the school's curriculum.

Mr. Ernst Papanek, executive director, I thank for his generosity and trust in giving me freedom to experiment and develop the art therapy program and for his continuous support of my work throughout. I am grateful to the board of directors and to the professional advisory board of Wiltwyck School for their support and interest. I wish especially to thank Mrs. Louis S. Weiss, president, for her active help.

For patient help and advice, I thank the editor, Dr. Molly Harrower, and the publishers.

To the late Dr. Ernst Kris I am deeply indebted for constructive criticism of the theoretical aspects of the book. I thank Dr. Annie Reich for guidance and suggestions at various stages of writing. Mrs. Christine Olden I thank for stimulating discussions and encouragement throughout the writing of the book. Before all, I am deeply grateful to Dr. Viola W. Bernard who was instrumental in obtaining for me the position of art therapist at Wiltwyck School and has supported my venture from the beginning. Without her enthusiasm and generous help this book would never have been written and published.

E. K.

CONTENTS

PREFACE vii
INTRODUCTION *By* VIOLA W. BERNARD, M.D. ix

Part I

INTRODUCTION TO ART THERAPY 5
    Definition 5
    Art and Society 7
    Psychology of the Artist and His Audience 10
    Sublimation 11
    Sublimation in Art 15
    Childhood and Art 18
    Conclusions for the Art Therapist 21

Part II

ART THERAPY IN A TREATMENT HOME 27
    The Children of Wiltwyck 27
    The Treatment Program 32
    The Art Therapy Program 35
    The Individual and the Group 41
        Raymond and His Sun 43
            Discussion 45
        Clyde's Horror Faces 47
        Martin, the Great Master 49

LEADERSHIP AND TRADITION 51
    Paul and John 52
        Conclusions 59
    Martin the Ethiopian 60
        Conclusions 63

Contents

KINGS, PRISONERS AND MONSTERS 66

    Kings 66

    Prisoners 71

        Discussion 79

    Monsters 81

        Paul and Clyde 83

        Clyde 85

        Harry, Master of Monsters 87

        Matthew 93

            Discussion 96

        The Little Boy's Monsters 98

        Edgar 99

        Harry's Later Development 101

            Discussion 102

REALITY RELATIONSHIP AND SUBJECT MATTER 109

THE LEARNING PROCESS 125

    Success and Growth 130

        Jacky 130

        Richard 132

    Perception and Skill 134

        Walter 134

        Ralph 135

    Pretense and Self-Acceptance 136

    Continuity and Growth 138

ART THERAPY AND AGGRESSION 141

    Aggressive Behavior 141

    Transformation of Aggression in Art 143

        Channeling of Aggression 144

        The Big Fist 145

    The Struggle with Aggression 148
        Escape and Denial 148
            The Fiery Tree 149
            Conclusions 152
        Counter Attack and Identification with
            the Aggressor 153
            Marwin 155
        Projection of Aggression 159
            Theodore, Caricaturist and Illustrator 159
            Building Fences around a Disturbance 164
        Self-Destructive Behavior 169

CONCLUSIONS 171

Part III

TWO CASE HISTORIES 175
    Frank 175
        Concluding Remarks 193
    Gordon 194
        Discussion 222

BIBLIOGRAPHY 227

INDEX 233

PART I

INTRODUCTION TO ART THERAPY

DEFINITION

ART THERAPY is a new profession. Its possibilities and limitations are not fully explored; even the term art therapy is not yet well defined. The distinctions between the use of art by psychologists and psychotherapists and the function of the art therapist seem confused.

Drawings and paintings of children and adults are used by psychotherapist and psychologist as an aid in diagnosis and therapy. They serve as a method of communication between therapist and patient and are valuable aids in the diagnosis and evaluation of personalities. In those cases art is used in conjunction with other methods. It is a tool among many others. Artistic values are of secondary importance. The art therapist also communicates with his students via the students' paintings and this communication has therapeutic value. He observes and evaluates his students' behavior and production, and his observation contributes to the understanding of the total personality of each of his students. But he is no psychotherapist, and it is not his function to interpret deep unconscious content to his students; nor are his observations a substitute for the psychologist's battery of tests.

The key to the understanding of the function of the art therapist lies in an understanding of his medium. The basic aim of the art therapist is to make available to disturbed persons the pleasures and satisfaction which creative work can give, and by his insight and therapeutic skill to make such experiences meaningful and valuable to the total personality. His medium, the plastic arts, is as old as mankind. Since human society has existed the arts have helped man to reconcile the eternal conflict between the individual's instinctual urges and the demands of society. Thus, all art is therapeutic in the broadest sense of the word. The artist who applies modern psychology in the field of art has to adapt his methods to the medium so that the therapeutic value of art is heightened and reinforced by the introduction of therapeutic thinking, not destroyed or weakened by the introduction of concepts and methods that might be incompatible with the inner laws of artistic creation. Thus, the art therapist combines several disciplines. He is at once artist, therapist, and teacher. To maintain a sound balance between his several functions is his greatest skill.

It is not always easy for the art therapist to reconcile the therapist's approach with his function as artist and teacher. In his function as the teacher who introduces disturbed children or adults into the realms of art, he has to be ready to accept the limitations of his students. He has to be interested in progress on any level. He has to be flexible enough to accept and understand a diversity of styles and to find ways of helping each student according to his individual needs. In his function as therapist he has to accept the unbeautiful manifestations of sexual and aggressive impulses in the raw, along with the results of confusions and incomplete sublimation, which his students may produce in their art. But this attitude of acceptance, which is essential in all therapy, must not dull the artist's capacity for discrimination. The teacher has to preserve his integrity as an artist in order to be able to distinguish between the fake and the genuine, between blocks and limitations, regressions and progress, superficial pretense and true sublimation, so that he can help each individual to reach whatever degree of artistic sublimation he is capable of in each instance. The art therapist's approach and goal varies with each individual. He plans and provides the conditions under which the creative process can take place and be pleasurable, and substitutes his knowledge and deliberate acts in any area where the individual is unable to function fully.

We may say that the art therapist is a specialist who combines the general qualification of being a competent artist with specialized skills in the field of psychotherapy and education. Wherever there is specialization there is the danger of distorted vision. Observations in a specialized field can be understood and evaluated only when they are seen as part of a dynamic whole. Art therapy can be understood best when it is seen as a specific field within the larger framework of art as a basic function of human society. In order to gain the necessary perspective we will have to begin with a presentation of the concepts which are the basis of our therapeutic approach.

ART AND SOCIETY

Since the time of the cave man, men have created configurations which serve as equivalents for life processes. We call those configurations works of art. The process by which this happens is as mysterious as all basic processes of life. Within the framework of this study it will not be possible to contribute much to the solution of the mystery; nor could we attempt even to touch on the wealth of thought and observation which exist on the subject. We have to limit ourselves strictly to presenting a few basic concepts in the hope that they may serve as a frame of reference and theoretical foundation for this study. As we are concerned with the plastic arts only, we will use the term art as an abbreviation for the longer, more correct term.

Art is a method of widening the range of human experiences by creating equivalents for such experiences. It is an area where experiences can be chosen, varied, and repeated at will. All artistic experiences take place in a world of symbols and conventions. It is an artificial world, but it has the power to evoke genuine emotions. The feeling of reality which works of art inspire is not necessarily related to their greater or lesser naturalistic verisimilitude, but depends on their power to evoke emotions within the audience. Indeed, creations which attempt too close an imitation of life forms, like wax works or artificial flowers, etc., cease to be art. Their value is at best sensational; basically they are unpleasant and evoke an uneasiness bordering on anxiety. One of the reasons for this uneasiness lies in the fact that here the distinction between the world of art and the world of reality is no longer clear. Works of art are enjoyed without guilt and anxiety only because they take place in an abstract framework of symbols and conventions which isolates them from reality, so that experiences which take place within this framework do not stimulate an urge for acting out. Because this is so, people can commit themselves to becoming involved in experiences which include deep unconscious content, and they can derive pleasure from them without fear that such adventures might impair their adjustment in reality or weaken their necessary defenses. Indeed the burden of repressions and denials is made easier by such artistic experiences.

In this respect works of art resemble dreams and daydreams. Dreams and fantasies often can be enjoyed with a minimum of guilt, even when they contain asocial and forbidden wishes, because the dreamer or daydreamer is certain that his fantasy will never become action. But fantasies and dreams are creations by the individual for his private use. They are formless, not meant for communication. Works of art, on the contrary, are formed, and their communication is pleasurable for the artist and his audience.

We find that form and communication belong together. The artist communicates with his audience in a language of symbols and conventions that are commonly understood. We can understand style and the changing of styles as the result of the interaction between the artist and his society. Thus, societies which change slowly, for example, the culture of old Egypt, produce a static, slow-changing style of art while our Western world, which for the last 2,000 years has been changing and developing with ever-increasing speed, has seen constant changes and transformations of style. When social changes take place so rapidly that the development of a style cannot keep pace with the changing state of society, art is apt to become formless. Left without a form in which to cast his message, the artist evolves his own private language and, with it, art ceases to be communication in the true sense of the word.

Thus art depends on society and contributes to society. We find that art adapts itself readily to the services of any field which happens to be an important factor in the cultural life of a people. According to the changing historical situation, art contributes to magic, religion, politics, the crafts, and many other fields. In some instances, such a state of amalgamation is reached that it becomes nearly impossible to distinguish the several elements. Magic and art form such a unity in totem poles or masks. Craft and art become one in medieval tapestry or in Indian pottery. We find that art enhances the effectiveness of any function to which it contributes while, in turn, art flourishes best as it contributes to other fields. But this holds true only as long as such a unity remains a productive, well-integrated factor in society. Art is exceedingly sensitive to social chasm, falsehood, and hypocrisy. For instance, religious art degenerates as soon as the religious life of a people declines. The quality of a craft declines when improved methods of production make the craft socially obsolete. Art becomes lifeless and empty when it serves an outdated, fossilized power system. In such historical situations art becomes isolated from its official social functions and is reduced to serving the individual. We can see such developments in the flourishing of Roman portraiture during a period when the official Roman art consisted of lifeless imitations of Greek sculpture, or towards the end of the Ninteenth Century when the term *l'art pour l'art* was coined to express the artist's isolation from society.

Because of the interdependence between art and society it often is difficult to recognize and to isolate the element of art within the fabric of society. But whatever the intricacies of each special situation might be, one factor remains constant: art contributes pleasure, pleasure chiefly derived from unconscious sources.

PSYCHOLOGY OF THE ARTIST AND HIS AUDIENCE

The statement which concludes the last section is too general for our use. At present we lack an understanding of the process by which artistic pleasure is generated and communicated. For a deeper understanding we would need a psychoanalysis of the artist and his audience, a task which is beyond the scope of this study and the competence of the author. All that we can attempt at this point is a brief presentation of a number of concepts which seem particularly relevant to the subject of this study. They will have to be abstractions which cannot do justice to the complexity and subtlety of life.

The artist is a person who has developed the capacity of resolving conflicts between the demands of his impulses and the demands of his superego, between reality and fantasy, through the creation of works of art. Through them he communicates his inner experiences to his audience in a sublimated culturally and socially productive form. The audience shares the artist's inner experiences on several levels, so that the audience experiences at once something of the primitive asocial impulse which the artist had to master, and the triumph of the successful transformation of the raw material into the work of art. In the ideal case, the spectator experiences a kind of minor miracle, as the artist's creative work makes it possible for the participant to achieve vicariously and with comparatively small effort a degree of sublimation which is ordinarily beyond the individual's reach. The success of a work of art with an audience depends, thus, not only on the artist's creative capacity, but equally on his audience's capacity and need for sublimation, and, with them, on many cultural and social factors. But before we investigate this problem any further, we have to define more clearly the concept of sublimation which we have been using all along.

SUBLIMATION

We call sublimation any process in which a primitive asocial impulse is transformed into a socially productive act, so that the pleasure in the achievement of the social act replaces the pleasure which gratification of the original urge would have afforded. For example, there is a beginning of sublimation when a small child prefers the joys of building a tower with his blocks to the aggressive pleasures of throwing them about, or finds the achievement of filling his spoon with food and finding his own mouth more rewarding than messing with his food. The child is stimulated towards such a choice by the mother's wishes, as she rewards achievement with love and admiration or shows disapproval of instinctual behavior. This lays the foundation for the development of the superego. But the achievement is performed by the child's ego. We may say that there is sublimation whenever instinctual behavior is replaced by a social act in such a manner that this change is experienced as a victory of the ego. Naturally the picture is not always clear. The child's feelings may be divided between a feeling of loss and defeat as an instinctual wish is relinquished, and a feeling of victory and pleasure as the ego achieves greater mastery over the environment and over the impulses. There is, at the root of all sublimation, an instinctual renunciation, and every step towards further sublimation is paid for by further renunciation. So that all sublimation contains an element of frustration and precariousness.

An instinct which spends itself through complete gratification will not be available for sublimation. Only when the original aim of the drive is blocked can the inherent energy become available for new purposes. However, this denial must not be too absolute. An instinct which is denied all direct gratification will be repressed so deeply that it will not be available for modification and transformation. For example, if the voyeuristic and aggressive sexual curiosity of a small child is frustrated entirely, the enjoyment of all visual impressions may become blocked, so that no receptiveness for the plastic arts and no talent for painting can develop. On the other hand, if the denial is not too absolute, the child might deflect its voyeuristic activities from their original aim, become a keen observer, develop a sensitivity for visual impressions, and may use his aggression in transforming the passive act of seeing into the active act of producing visual images. The original curiosity will always continue to exist (all artists are voyeurs to some degree), but it will lose its singleminded infantile obsessiveness as more and more energy is invested in creative work. Naturally this outcome does not depend only on the degree of the denial, but equally on the love and admiration which the child obtains for his creative efforts. It depends, last but not least, on the child's talent—that elusive quality which makes certain paths of sublimation seem easy and natural, even inevitable, for some individuals, so that a minimum of encouragement suffices in making them productive, while others seem to have little capacity in the same direction.

Sublimation, then, is a process in which an instinctual aim is denied direct gratification. The original aim is replaced by a new, socially acceptable aim through a process which includes repression and reaction formation. The instinctual energy which is not discharged becomes, at least in part, available to the ego, is used in the development of skills and accomplishments which give the individual greater mastery over his environment and improve his capacity for positive object relationship so that he becomes a more valuable member of society. The gratification which this accomplishment affords replaces instinctual gratification. The process begins early in life, before the establishment of the superego. It is an important factor in ego and superego formation.

With maturity and the establishment of the superego, sublimation becomes the ego's most economical method of reconciling the demands of the superego with instinctual demands. As the ego succeeds in forming a superstructure through which forbidden sexual and aggressive drives can find some measure of gratification through socially productive acts, gratification becomes possible with the approval of the superego. The ego succeeds in its function as an integrating force and is rewarded by a feeling of peace and achievement. Pleasure is gained from superego and id, two forces that are ordinarily antagonistic. This reconciliation is not static. It is a continuous process of maintaining a balance between conflicting forces. It requires a continuous expenditure of energy and produces a state of tension which is never relaxed entirely. Finally, this balance does not include the individual's inner world alone, but, for ultimate peace of mind, society has to approve of the individual's efforts. Naturally our description has been schematic. Sublimation seldom exists in a pure, unmixed state. We find in every individual a mixture of repressions, reaction formations, neurotic symptoms, and other mechanisms along with genuine sublimation.

Any life process seems complex and confusing when it is described in words. Our detailed description of the mechanisms of sublimation makes the process appear unduly complicated and difficult to achieve. Granted that human beings are by nature complicated, and that the ego's task is not an easy one, sublimation seems to be the most natural or rewarding function of the ego. It is the ego's task to reconcile and integrate conflicting forces with a minimum of displeasure. Through sublimation, pleasure is gained without arousing excessive anxiety from within or hostility from without. The achievement of this rare state of balance constitutes the ego's greatest victory. Indeed human beings are so addicted to this kind of pleasure that they suffer intense frustration if channels for sublimation are blocked.

Our work with children who have been deprived in early childhood of experiences which lead to sublimation or later have been deprived of physical and emotional opportunities for sublimation, shows that frustration in this area leads to disturbances that are as serious and as painful as those that are the result of denials of instinctual gratification. And, this cannot surprise us if we consider that ultimately only aggressive or autoerotic gratifications can be enjoyed without some vestiges of sublimation. All positive interpersonal relationships are bound up with the modification of instinctual behavior for the sake of the relationship.

This digression into the psychology of sublimation in general leaves many questions unanswered, but we have to return to the special problem of sublimation in the plastic arts.

SUBLIMATION IN ART

Artistic sublimation begins as the artist replaces the impulse to act out his fantasies with the act of creating equivalents for his fantasies through visual images. Those creations become true works of art only as the artist succeeds in making them meaningful to others. The complete act of sublimation, then, consists in the creation of visual images for the purpose of communicating to a group very complex material which would not be available for communication in any other form. Form and content become an inseparable whole.

The need for this kind of communication has many sources. For one, there is the repressed material itself which pushes to the surface and demands fulfillment. Then, there is man's paramount narcissism which cannot suffer the fact that any part of his person has to remain hidden and unloved, so that he is moved to exhibit his hidden self through his creations. In doing this the artist sacrifices part of his primitive narcissism by transferring his love onto his creations, which he endows with all the beauty and perfection he is capable of so that they may be admired and loved as he wishes to be loved himself. The final reason, which embraces all the other reasons, is man's great need to overcome the isolation which is part of human life. Through art man can partake in the inner world of other men without losing his integrity as an individual, and find security and pleasure in this communion.

We can see that works of art always remain emotionally charged. Conflict is formed and contained, but only partly neutralized. Art differs here from most other forms of sublimation.

For instance, when aggressive energy is sublimated in constructive work like carpentry, the result will not be a monument to the carpenter's aggression, but a useful, emotionally neutral object like a table or a chair. Or, the result of the scientist's curiosity will not be an expression of this curiosity, but objective truth. But every work of art contains a core of conflicting drives which give it life and determine form and content to a large degree.

For example, all great portraits contain the artist's intuitive knowledge and understanding of his subject along with an interpretation of the subject's position in society, so that the spectator who may never have seen the living person obtains through the portrait the intuitive knowledge and awareness of another human being. The portrait, then, is born of the desire to possess and preserve the essence of a human being. The instinctual root of this desire is the small child's wish to incorporate and devour the beloved object. It finds its earliest cultural expression in cannibalism, head hunting, the smoking of heads, embalming practices, etc. In those primitive forms love and care are exercised in the preservation and the adornment of the trophy, but the initial possession is possible only through an act of destruction. In portrait painting intuitive understanding, observation, and technical skill replace those primitive methods. So that, in the ideal case, far from feeling threatened and robbed by the artist, the person whose portrait is being painted becomes more aware of himself and feels more fully alive as some of his essential being is eternalized in the picture.

The energies of primitive libidinal and aggressive impulses are used in the developing of technical skill, power of observation, and depth of understanding. But the basic need for possession and incorporation remains active and is fulfilled, although in a transformed manner. Indeed the depth of intuitive knowledge which is the essence of great portraiture could not be obtained without the help of those unconscious wishes. In the artist's compassionate or merciless, or dispassionately objective interpretation of the individual we can feel an echo of the mixture of love and aggression which is at the root of it all. And we can observe an unconscious awareness of those processes in the reaction of the public towards portraits, which often is a mixture of awe and revulsion, admiration and distrust towards artist and portrait.

This digression into the psychology of portrait painting illustrates the artist's precarious position. While his craft demands a strong ego capable of great perseverance, concentration, and precision, his raw materials are untamed instinctual drives, so that in order to remain creative the artist has to remain sensitive to the unconscious forces within himself and in others, and has to permit his impulses to come close to the surface. This explains why we often find in artists the highest level of sublimation coexisting with instinctual and impulsive behavior. The balance between sublimation, repression, and instinctual gratification varies with individual artists. The artist may be impulse-ridden or ascetic; he may be a slow, steady worker or alternate between periods of heightened productivity and blocking. But a certain tolerance towards direct instinctual gratification in some form or other seems inevitable. A person who has established very rigorous, inflexible defenses against his impulses, or a person who has resolved his conflicts so well that there remains not much pressure from the unconscious, will not become an artist.

CHILDHOOD AND ART

There is, however, one period in life when most people are artists to some degree. If given the opportunity, most children in latency and prepuberty will paint pictures of great expressiveness and originality. We do not know all the reasons which make this age so favorable for the plastic arts, but it seems that the balance of forces between 6 and 12 years is especially conducive to artistic expression. The ego at this time already is capable of concentrated effort and the mastery of a medium like clay or paint. But defenses and repressions are not yet firmly established, and the reality principle has not gained complete ascendance over the pleasure principle. There exists a constant need to master impulses and fantasies through the creating of equivalents in art.

This readiness for artistic creation may remain dormant if the environment does not encourage its expression.

That the capacity is latent during those periods, is borne out by the great eagerness with which most children from 6 years up to 11 or 12 years of age respond when opportunity and encouragement for artistic expression are offered, and by the rapid development of their latent artistic faculties which follows so frequently.

We may assume that in the adult artist certain mechanisms from this period of childhood are preserved. And it seems probable that the amateur's enjoyment of art is facilitated by the fact that a period of latent capacity for artistic creation is part of everybody's childhood. Naturally we must not oversimplify. We can not equate the artistic personality with the latency period, or reduce the complexity of the adult creative process to the level of children's art.

To appreciate the distance which separates children's art from the art of adults we may have to recall how confused most children are by adult art. As a rule they are bored in art galleries. They prefer trashy illustrations to the greatest masterpieces, and, even when they happen to like a good picture, this liking will depend mostly on subject matter or other features and not on artistic values. Only with the beginning of puberty comes the gradual awareness of our artistic heritage.

But the same children who have no judgment for great art will be excellent judges of the art of their contemporaries. Children who paint together soon develop a remarkable degree of understanding and appreciation for each other's work, so that often their judgment will be more penetrating than the observations of adults. And this is not surprising if one considers how much the understanding of art depends on a common cultural and emotional situation.

Although children live in the same cultural environment as their elders, they also live in a world of their own, and their art expresses this world-within-our-world. The adult who tries to understand and evaluate children's art can be compared to an anthropologist who is studying the art of another culture. With practice and increasing knowledge the outsider may learn to empathize with a culture and eventually arrive at a genuine appreciation of its art. But he will remain an outsider—the spontaneous mutual understanding which exists between the artist and his cultural group remains beyond his reach.

Of course, a group of children is not a cultural unit as each child belongs to its family unit. Children's art depends on guidance and help from adults, and children naturally crave the adults' appreciation of their art, as they need appreciation for all accomplishments. Thus pictures are often given as presents to beloved adults. But, while adults are frequently the recipients of children's art, they are not the child artist's audience—if we continue to define as audience the individual or the group who vicariously shares the artist's inner experiences. For instance, a mother to whom her little son presents his many pictures of cars, may be very pleased with the presents. She may appreciate decorative qualities or be impressed and proud of the child's skill and observation. If she is familiar with modern psychology, she might also correctly interpret their symbolic meaning. But she could not possibly be stimulated by the paintings to experiencing vicariously her little son's passion for cars, or his castration fear and his methods of reassuring himself. Thus, with the best of will, she cannot be a fully appreciative audience, while her little son's schoolmates, who are in the same developmental stage, will intuitively appreciate the inner meaning of his paintings.

CONCLUSIONS FOR THE ART THERAPIST

The general ideas which have been presented cannot be used as answers to the many practical questions which are involved in the conducting of an art therapy program, but a number of ideas which may guide the art therapist's general approach can be formulated.

The art therapist assists in an act of integration and synthesis which is performed by the ego. Also, since all art is communication, he assists in a social act. This communication is not meant for the therapist alone, as in individual therapy. It is directed more generally to any individual or group who is ready to receive the message. We can see that the therapeutic situation would be incomplete without such an audience. Naturally there will be cases where the therapist may be the only kind of audience which the student is able to tolerate, and the art therapist's understanding is in every case essential as a first step in communication, but the ultimate goal would be to help the student towards communication with a larger group.

If one is working with adults, a dilemma arises; although the students are to some extent in the emotional situation of artists, their productions can seldom be considered to have value as works of art. The art therapist in his role as representative of reality has to maintain in his students the awareness that they cannot aspire to be recognized as artists in the world at large. The audience for the adult's production will be limited to the therapist or to other students who are in a similar situation, or to the student's immediate circle of family and friends. So there will always be an artificial quality to this aspect of art therapy. The art therapist will have to help the student to accept this fact as part of the artificial symbolic quality of the therapeutic situation.

When the art therapist is working with disturbed children no such difficulty exists. Here the difference between artist and laymen is only a matter of degree. The children constitute an ideal and natural audience for each other. But this will be true only if the whole community has an opportunity to create, so that no artificial distinction between a painting and a non-painting population is created.

An effective art therapy program in a children's community depends on a satisfying and creative art program for the whole community. Indeed the distinction between art teaching and art therapy is often hard to draw, so that the art therapist ideally should be in charge of the total program. Where this would be impracticable, and an art teacher and an art therapist have to work side by side, it will be important that their basic approach be alike.

We can see that the art therapist who works in a children's community has, besides his function as individual therapist, a function also as social therapist who works with the community as a whole. He acts as moderator and guide of public opinion and creates a cultural atmosphere in which the arts can flourish. The therapeutic relationship to the student remains less intimate than in psychotherapy. The transference which is established between art therapist and student centers around the student's work. It does not become the core of the therapeutic situation as in psychotherapy, but remains subordinate to the task of making the student productive.

While the art therapist assists the student's creative efforts, he will be careful not to disturb the creative process by interference beyond a certain depth. Since large areas of the ego are unconscious, the process by which libidinal and aggressive energy become available to the ego remains largely unconscious. Therefore it is not necessary and, indeed, not advisable to bring the raw material too close to the surface. This would disturb a process which cannot take place on a conscious level alone. Such an interference may encourage acting out on a primitive level which could not be handled constructively in art therapy. Or it may result in the total repression of the material so that it would no longer be available for creative work.

The art therapist's main field of action remains the process of sublimation wherein the material undergoes that final transformation by which it is formed into tangible visual images, and the peculiar fusion between reality and fantasy, between the unconscious and the conscious, which we call art is reached. At this point the art therapist assists the process by substituting his skill and insight where the student's own resources fail. Since the artistic quality of the production is an indication of the depth and strength of sublimation, the art therapist will encourage a high artistic level of performance within the limitations of the student's talent.

Because the need for art therapy arises from inner difficulties, art therapy will terminate as the individual becomes less disturbed. In the adult artistic creation will usually cease at this point. Occasionally art therapy may awaken a dormant talent, and the student may continue to use art as a means of expression. But this development is beyond the field of art therapy and belongs to the realms of pure art.

PART II

ART THERAPY IN THE TREATMENT HOME

THE CHILDREN OF WILTWYCK

WILTWYCK SCHOOL is an interracial, nonsectarian treatment home for disturbed boys of greater New York, ages 8 to 13. They are referred to the school by various agencies. The majority of the boys referred by the children's courts have committed asocial acts. Other children are referred by the Department of Welfare because of neglect. Some children come from institutions or foster homes where they failed to adjust, and a number of children are admitted on petition of their parents. Before admission, each child is observed and tested. Only those children who are too disturbed to profit simply by removal from a harmful environment and placement in good foster homes or boarding schools are admitted to the treatment home. The school is not equipped to care for children who need hospitalization or the safety of a home which provides continuous close supervision. Children whose I.Q.'s are below 75 are admitted only when there are reasons to believe that their potential intelligence is higher than their performance.

Within those limits Wiltwyck School's population reflects the enormous cultural, religious, and racial variety of greater New York's population. The existing inequalities and added tensions in the lives of racial minorities are reflected in the high percentage of Negro and Puerto Rican children at the school. The fact that only boys are admitted constitutes a serious default of the present treatment program. Lack of funds have held up plans for conversion to coeducation up to date.

Wiltwyck's population is, then, not homogenous culturally. Also, since Wiltwyck does not specialize in any one type of disturbance, the children's behavior, their symptoms, and needs vary. Only the relatively narrow age range of 8 to 13 assures a certain uniformity. Even there the actual behavior oscillates easily between the immaturity of the 2 to 3 year old child, and the worldly shrewdness of the adult delinquent.

Whatever the individual differences may be, the children have one thing in common: all come from an environment which in some way or other has failed to fulfill some of their basic needs and is helpless in the face of the resulting disturbance. At the time of their admission to Wiltwyck School the situation has become intolerable to children, parents, and society. This impasse may have been reached for any number of reasons. Constitutional factors may have made the upbringing of the child difficult and may have burdened the child's parents beyond their capacities. The confusion and shock which accompany readjustment to another culture and environment may have disrupted the equilibrium within a family of Puerto Ricans, or of Negroes from the rural South, or European immigrants. The absence of a father, emotional disturbance in the family, alcoholism, illness, death, and poverty may have brought about an intolerable situation. As a rule the severe disturbances that are treated at Wiltwyck are the result of an accumulation of many serious difficulties.

Whatever the etiology of each case may be, by the time of his admission each child harbors within himself a deep core of unfulfilled needs, fears, and bitterness, which distort and stunt his growth and make him unable to fulfill the demands of society. Upon this weak foundation the mores of New York street life have left their imprint. This common experience gives a superficial similarity to the children's behavior.

From an early age on, the little boy's primary preoccupation has been self-defense. On the street the 4 to 5 year old must already hold his own against the other children. The little boy is forced to develop a truculent, masculine front at a period of his life when his need for support and protection is still imperative, when overwhelming fears and anxieties create a constant need for reassurance, and defeat is still a terrifying threat to his precarious masculinity.

Because the battle for survival begins so early, the child can cope with it only through primitive mechanisms of denial, delusions of grandeur, and, above all, through the mobilization of tremendous hostility and aggression. The child who is not able to override his need for protection may admit defeat from the beginning and try to avoid danger by accepting a passive feminine role towards the other boys. His suppressed hostility may then be turned against his own self, and a passive, masochistic pattern may develop.

In either case the greatest danger is the possibility of a fixation on an infantile level, just because independence and self-assertion had to develop precociously and needs for support and reassurance remain unfulfilled. The whole area of self-assertion and competition may remain permanently charged with primitive sexual conflict. The development of genuine self-reliance and a mature masculinity will then be blocked, not only in the passive homosexual child, but also in the aggressive child whose masculinity never quite outgrows the level of the truculent, insecure little boy. A stable, reassuring family life usually prevents such long-lasting effects. But when the defensive frame of mind which the child maintains on the outside feeds on deep hurts in the child's inner life, there may be lasting disturbances. Then each aggressive act encountered on the street finds an echo in the devastating rage which the child feels at home, and street battles are charged with the irrational blind hate of the frustrated infant. In an atmosphere that is overcharged with aggression, there is no place for the complex process by which an ego is formed. There is not much possibility for learning to resolve conflict by more mature methods, and the child's personality remains unstructured and impulsive. The inclination for temper tantrums, for irrational hate, and anger may even become assets, so that secondary gain may be drawn from the symptom. The loss of feelings of hate may result in diminished capacity for self-defense and become dangerous to the child who continues to live in an environment where the ability to fight ferociously means protection from danger.

The child who is burdened with conflict and frustration in the family, and harassed by the necessity for vigilant self-defense on the street, has little energy left for learning and growth. The first years of elementary school often mark the point where the child and his environment are first confronted with the full impact of his disturbance and inadequacies. Elementary school presupposes in the 6 to 7 years old a personality which is consolidated to a point. The child should have formed the core of his ego and superego and should have obtained a certain measure of control over his impulses. Within the next few years the child is ready to incorporate the basic moral code and the heritage of knowledge of his society. The child whose personality is not sufficiently formed, whose ego is still at the mercy of its impulses, will fail at this task. Just as the young adult is faced at the close of adolescence with the facts of his particular sexual personality as it emerges from the adolescent turmoil, the child of school age and his parents are faced with the results of the first 6 fateful years of his life, and early failure at school is almost always a traumatic experience. In the overcrowded, understaffed classrooms of New York, a disturbed child has little chance of being helped. Failure at school usually means failure at learning how to read, and, if the child does not acquire this basic technique most other avenues of academic learning remain closed to him. The child then never experiences the widening of horizons and the elation of an increasing understanding and mastery of the world which should be the great experience of childhood. School and learning, which can become a strong steadying and healing factor in a disturbed child's life become instead another source of conflict and bitterness.

By the time of their admission to Wiltwyck most of the children have behind them a destructive early childhood, several years of a dangerous life on the streets and at least 2 years of failure at school. Naturally this is a somewhat sweeping statement. Not all factors are present in each child's life, and the role which each single factor may have played in the child's development differs from child to child. But anybody familiar with low income groups, especially with minority groups, in large cities will recognize problems that exist throughout the United States.*

---

*For a deeper understanding of those problems Fritz Redl's excellent book, *Children Who Hate,* gives an inspired, penetrating analysis of the disturbed delinquent city child. His histories are extremes. The children at Wiltwyck are as a rule not quite as disturbed as those described by Redl, but basically the majority of Wiltwyck's population are of the same type.

THE TREATMENT PROGRAM

Wiltwyck School maintains a large staff. Backgrounds, nationalities, and age groups among staff members vary greatly. Success in treatment depends on teamwork, mutual respect, and unity among staff members. The executive director, the resident director and his assistant, and the director of social services, provide the philosophy and leadership necessary for the functioning of the total treatment program. The Board of Directors is responsible for the agencies policy and budget. The services of a professional advisory board contributes to the high professional standards of the program.

Wiltwyck has no cottage parents. The children live in groups of 10 to 12, with two counselors for each group. For deeply disturbed children it seems advisable to create a basic situation which is emotionally more neutral than a family situation, so that, the new relationships which the child forms at the school may not be burdened from the beginning with the whole weight of the child's family conflicts. In some cases the child's home situation may be so far removed from the conventionally accepted family setting that living in an artificial family may bring those discrepancies so constantly to the child's mind that it may create an intolerable division of alliance. Or, the resemblance to a family situation might induce a child to transfer his home conflict with full force onto the cottage parents, thus creating a deadlock for treatment. In the course of treatment such problems should be met gradually, and ultimately the child should be ready to live again in a family, at home or in a foster home.

The counselor takes the role of the cottage parent in matters of routine, but his responsibilities go beyond it. He shares the boys' life more actively than a cottage parent would; he plans and conducts activities and acts as a leader and guide to his group. Thus the general atmosphere at the school, the success or non-success of all treatment depends ultimately on the devotion and skill of the young men and women in whose hands is the immediate basic task of rehabilitation and reorientation of the boys. Their work is guided and supervised by senior counselors and head counselors, old practitioners who combine psychological insight with years of experience at counseling. They maintain a close relationship to the boys, so that they are in a position to help them at times when they are unable to tolerate a group situation. They protect the children from each other, settle arguments, and in general symbolize to the boys justice and law of a kind they can accept and trust.

The boy's link with his family and with the world at large is his social worker. The social workers' caseload is light enough to permit them to work intensively with the children and with their families. All social workers are trained in psychiatric social work and able to do a certain amount of psychotherapy. They work under the guidance of social work supervisors with access to psychiatric consultation. The social workers evaluate their children's progress at the school. At their request children may be given additional help from the agency's professional staff. In cooperation with the staff they plan for the child's discharge and his future life. Unless the child is discharged to another agency, the child remains in aftercare, and his social worker continues to give his services to the child and his family as long as it is needed. Social services are co-ordinated by the director of social work. Additional clinical services are provided by the agency's psychiatrist and treatment by psychotherapists, group therapists, and psychologists.

The professional staff also includes a registered nurse, remedial reading teachers, psychologist, a dancing and rhythms teacher, and the art therapist.* The Board of Education maintains an elementary school on the campus.

The treatment program depends upon the establishment of a setting in which there is no brutality, no coercion through fear, and where the demands made on the child do not exceed his capacities, so that the child may learn to like and to trust the adults who take care of him and to enjoy the new life experiences which the school offers. The difficulties in creating such a setting lie in the fact that many of the children are unable to accept discipline and order of any kind so that even the most reasonable demand is often felt as an imposition to which the child might react with any amount of hostility. Street life has established among the children a pattern of brutality, bullying, and rape which makes group life frought with friction and dangers. The children are unaccustomed to organized activities, they have not developed the skill and patience necessary for creative work, and they lack the discipline and code of fair play which is necessary in sports.

The dilemma which confronts everyone consists of the fact that all re-education depends upon the establishment of positive relationships and trust between child and educator, and upon the satisfying experiences which he can provide for the child. Educational work cannot proceed unless the children are protected from each other and unless a certain regularity and serenity can be established within the group. The problem of avoiding chaos and bloodshed without resorting to rigid discipline or

---

*New services are added as the budget permits.

corporal punishment continuously taxes the ingenuity and patience of all workers.

The greatest help in all treatment is the children's inner needs. Even though early experiences in human relationships may have been frustrating and disastrous, their overwhelming need for adult care and affection urges children to try again and again to find people who can fulfill those needs. Ambivalence and distrust may cause many attempts at establishing relationships to fail, but the resilience of childhood makes it possible for both adults and children to tolerate breakdowns and failures until enduring relationships are formed.

THE ART THERAPY PROGRAM

The art therapist's function in the community is twofold. She works with the individual child and with the community as a whole. Her success or non-success in individual therapy depends in part on her success in making art an integral part of the cultural life of the school. The art program is accessible to every child. Participation depends on the children's needs and wishes. Children with a special affinity to art are given extra time, space, and attention according to their needs. The children's work is exhibited regularly and the exhibition is kept up-to-date so that it truly reflects the artistic production within the group.

The art program provides roughly a minimum of 1 hour of art per week for every child, with a maximum of about 6 hours for those who are most interested. However, when the need arises, the passionate painter may spend as much as 10 or 12 hours a week in the art room. A record time was reached by Martin who began by painting an apple at 9:30 A.M. The painting developed into a close-up of a section of an apple tree, full of apples and leaves, with a bird sitting among the apples. With time out for meals, Martin spent the whole day in the art room, completing his painting at 7:30 P.M.

The art therapist is at the school 3 days a week. During this time art sessions are held from 9:30 A.M. to 5:30 P.M. During school hours each classroom has one art session of 1 hour and 10 minutes per week. As the need arises, children may spend additional time in the art room whenever this is feasible.

After school hours, from 3:30 to 5:30 P.M., all children are offered a free choice of several activities. The group that attends art at this time consists of those who have chosen art in preference to any other activity. In this manner children can spend additional time in the art room on their own initiative. There are, of course, instances when children are encouraged to come to art more often, or when a child is urged to seek other means of expression besides art. In general it seems impossible to gauge the fluctuations in the need for art therapy among 100 boys accurately, and leaving the initiative to the children seems the safest way of providing each boy with the number of art sessions he needs.

The boys' finished work is kept in the artroom in individual folders. They have access to their work during art sessions. The children are free to take pictures home, give them away as presents, or eliminate pictures.

The art material consists of paper of all sizes, including a roll of brown wrapping paper which allows the creation of heroic-size murals, poster paint and charcoal, and pencils and sketchbooks for those boys who are interested in sketching the world around them.

Finger paint and oil paint are not used in art therapy, although finger paint is used in individual sessions by social workers and psychotherapists. The reasons for those limitations of materials are chiefly practical. Finger paint seems useful in working with very infantile children who are in the process of making the transition from anal play to a more sublimated form of expression, or for children who need to recapture infantile pleasures which they have missed. As treatment proceeds finger paint would eventually be replaced by material which permits a more structured form of expression. Oil paint, on the other hand, can be used successfully only by children who are capable of working on one picture for a considerable length of time and with a fair amount of skill. Finger paint, then, would be associated in the children's minds with an immature, babyish kind of work, while oil paint becomes associated with advanced, grown-up painting.

The physical setup of the school is such that any consistent separation of groups is impracticable. All art activities on the campus take place in full view of the whole population. For deprived children material things are especially loaded emotionally, so that any inequalities in the use of materials tremendously increases jealousies and tensions among the group. If only a small group of children were privileged to use oil paint, those children would become a target of hostility and their materials and pictures would be in danger of being destroyed by jealous schoolmates, while giving the material to all children would be a frustrating experience for those who are not ready to handle the difficult medium. The same kind of dilemma appears in the use of finger paint. Limiting it to those children who could use it therapeutically would single them out as babyish, unskilled boys. Giving the medium to all would mean seducing children to regress who already have reached a higher stage of sublimation. It seems better, therefore, to give the children a medium which can be used both ways. Tempera paint can be used by the infantile child for all sorts of messing and experimenting, while the talented child can use the same medium on a high artistic level without frustration.

With a population of ages 8 to 13, the art program is more or less universally accepted by the younger children. Among the 12 and 13 year old boys there is more of a division between those whose interest in art deepens and those who lose interest as they grow older.

To give a general idea of the average participation, during the years 1953 and 1954, there was, among 95 to 100 boys, an average of 10 to 15 boys who did not participate at all, an average of 18 to 22 who attended frequently, and a core of 5 to 8 unusually talented boys whose chief interest was art. The remaining boys participated regularly at the rate of approximately 3 hours per month.

Winning the children's interest is no serious problem, and it is usually possible, in spite of all emotional ups and downs, to establish a positive working relationship between teacher and individual child. The greatest difficulty in establishing a good art program is the children's hostility against each other. The children approach art, as everything else, in a spirit of mutual distrust and hate. Each painter sees in the other one a potential enemy and rival. Sharing the teacher's attention, sharing space and material, constitutes a problem. Fighting for material becomes totally irrational, so that two children may fight tooth and nail for the possession of a tray full of paints, while a whole tableful of identical trays is in plain view. The children's feeling for their painting is ambivalent. Their natural pride in the work of their hands is outbalanced by a general feeling of unworthiness. The contempt and hate in which they hold themselves finds expression in their great readiness to destroy their own work and the work of others. Their low self-esteem makes them distrust their original ideas and forms of expression, so that they have a great need for conformity and a conventional kind of perfection. Talented children are not easily tolerated. In a sense, almost any unusual production—good or bad—is viewed with distrust.

Fortunately those negative factors are counterbalanced by the innate creativeness of childhood. Especially when there is a dormant talent, the children find themselves soon carried away by the magnetism of creative work, and with it new feelings and needs arise which contradict their old patterns. Success in painting strengthens the boys' self-esteem and makes them more ready to accept themselves and to accept others. The boys find that they need an appreciative audience for their pictures. They are inclined to admire each other's work, and, the once-hated rival becomes the admired leader. As they discover the pleasures of creative work the children find that their destructiveness and hostility becomes a burden and hindrance in the enjoyment of art sessions. They begin to long for a quiet productive time, undisturbed by bickering and battles. But even when the longing for better conditions is awakened, change of behavior remains difficult. Any change deep enough to be of therapeutic value would be based on the boys' identification with each other, and on their identification with the teacher. But a life of vigilant self-defense where everyone fights a lonely battle against the rest of the world has made the children into isolated individuals who have not learned to identify. Thus, even with the best of will, the children are unable to maintain a spirit conducive to creative work without the therapist's aid. She has to foresee difficulties, calm tempers, help the frustrated, and pick up the pieces after each breakdown. Through such experiences identification with the therapist and her values is gradually formed. This process will be analyzed in detail in another chapter.

Identification among the boys is facilitated by their paintings. Communication through their pictures is a new experience which breaks through the children's isolation and creates a new kind of understanding among them. But art sessions alone do not suffice in forming identification between the children. A wider, more neutral ground is needed, one removed from the irritation and frustration of the creative act itself. An exhibition of their paintings is the most effective medium in establishing a spirit of mutual acceptance and identification. In setting up such an exhibition we are confronted with the ever-recurring problem—how to provide a constructive experience for the children in spite of their destructive behavior.

At first it seemed almost impossible to find wall space that was safe from the children's destructiveness and still accessible to all. The only area which fulfilled those requirements was the dining room. Mealtimes also seemed a good occasion for contemplation and enjoyment of pictures. Soon every inch of wall space was covered with paintings. The over-all effect is beautiful and stimulating to adults and children alike. The exhibition is never static, new pictures go up as soon as they are produced. The children watch for changes, discuss them during meals, and are amused and stimulated by the over-all effect beyond their conscious perception of individual paintings. Thus the children's paintings fulfill the social function of art—to inspire and to give pleasure to the community, and, in spite of individual jealousies and hostilities, the boys have a constant and appreciative audience for their work.

The walls of the dining room are neutral ground. The very multitude of pictures has a leveling influence on individual feelings. The fact that pictures are hung side by side makes it more possible for the children to identify with the good work which is being done at their school and be proud of it. Boys who are discouraged with their work often can accept their paintings once they are hanging in the dining room, as if the paintings were redeemed by participating in the exhibition. The mutual identification and acceptance which the exhibition awakens carries over into art sessions and helps to neutralize jealousies and destructiveness. Since the children are reasonably sure that their work will not be destroyed and will be appreciated, they can allow themselves to identify more fully with their paintings. The re-education of children who newly enter the school becomes easier through the general atmosphere of pride in and acceptance of paintings.

THE INDIVIDUAL AND THE GROUP

Artistic creation is always both a private experience and a public event. Art sessions are held in groups of six to ten because painting in a group creates an intense, inspiring working atmosphere for each individual. But no attempt is made at creating specific group situations. During art sessions each child is engrossed in his own work. But in a subtle way the creative work of each painter is influenced by the artistic output of the whole community. Just as in society at large, the talented individuals give form and direction to the production of the group. Subject matter, style, the very atmosphere in the art room is influenced by the personalities of the leaders who emerge successively as the population slowly changes. Providing that it is not dictatorial or sterile, leadership does not hinder the development of individuality and self-fulfillment. Talented children act as catalysts around which the production of the group crystallizes. They provide their less gifted schoolmates with forms in which to cast their individual message.

The art therapist cannot create talent, nor can she influence the nature and quality of her students' gifts. It is her role to see to it that every kind of talent finds fulfillment, that variety of style and temperament are respected, and that no individual is forced into forms which are detrimental to his personality. She sees to it, that battles of factions, intolerance, over-evaluation of fashionable trends and the resulting impoverishment of the arts, which so frequently happens in society at large, are not permitted to develop beyond a point. Among children who do not speak easily actions carry more weight than words. The loving care with which paintings are exhibited, the trouble the therapist is ready to take in hanging, re-hanging, and preserving their pictures proves to the children that the paintings are valuable to the teacher. This forms the basis for the children's own attitude towards their work.

In this spirit the therapist accepts any painting which constitutes a child's genuine effort, however primitive. The line is drawn at products which are the conscious expressions of contempt and regression on part of the child. In other words, an immature child's effort which results in masses of brown and dirty colors may be exhibited because it constitutes the beginning of his development as a painter. A more mature child's ugly smearings would constitute an expression of contempt, which could not be accepted. If such anti-paintings were placed side by side with pictures, it would mean an insult to those children who have made a creative effort, whose paintings would be placed on one level with anal aggression in the raw. Downright pornographic pictures and pictures that are meant to hurt or ridicule another person also are not exhibited. Those limitations protect the exhibition from becoming a battleground for mutual aggression and contempt. Otherwise every effort is made to comply with each child's wishes concerning the choice of his pictures, the length of time they are left hanging, placement, and grouping of his paintings, etc.

The following case histories illustrate how picture hanging may become therapeutically meaningful.

Raymond and His Sun

Raymond came to Wiltwyck at the age of 10. He was an undersized boy, intelligent, solitary, and very much on the defensive. He never fitted into a group, but formed a strong attachment to one of the head counselors, a tall athletic man. Although he remained an oddity, the isolated, depressed child found ways of existing at the school and getting some degree of happiness and benefit from the environment.

During his first year Raymond did not paint. When he finally attempted painting at 11 years of age his concepts were on a 3 to 4 year old level. There was much general confusion, especially his paintings of people showed many bizarre elements. Soon his chief interest became painting the sun, moon, and stars. Once he drew the smiling face of a sun with charcoal on a large sheet of paper (Fig. 1). Then he covered the whole paper with bright yellow paint, and drew the smiling face again swiftly with black paint, using the still faintly visible charcoal lines as a guide. By some miracle born of the speed and simplicity of the execution and the deep emotional significance of the theme, the picture was expressive and beautiful in spite of the boy's limitations as a painter.

When the picture was hung in a fittingly central position for a sun, Raymond was delighted. Shortly afterwards Raymond went to live with his parents. He returned to Wiltwyck within 2 months after experiencing a total rejection at home. By this time the picture had

Fig. 1. Size, 18 x 24 inches, tempera.

been taken down. Upon his return the art therapist offered to hang the picture up again. Raymond did not want it back, but immediately set about painting a new sun. In his eagerness he produced a whole series of suns and gave a number of them away as presents. When his new sun was hung in the same place as the old one, Raymond was elated. He showed it to every staff member. Hanging the sun signified to Raymond his reintegration into the community and his acceptance of his return to Wiltwyck School. Subsequently Raymond returned home twice. Each time he came back after another rejection from the parents, and twice again a sun was taken down and replaced by a new one. His subsequent suns were never as beautiful as the first one, probably because the rejections at home had left a scar, but also, because miracles like the creation of the first sun can seldom be repeated.

When he was 13 the sun ceased to have so much significance for Raymond. By then he had mastered the human figure and was busy painting ladies and gentlemen. His paintings were still infantile, but less bizarre. Raymond's last sun no longer needed to be hung at the center of the dining room. He found a place in a corner and it eventually was taken down to make space for another picture.

Discussion

Almost any child's self-esteem would be heightened by public display of his work. The emotional significance of Raymond's sun goes deeper. The painting expressed Raymond's personality fully, including the bizarre, odd streak. This would not have been possible if Raymond had been urged to paint a nice, conventional picture. To succeed in this Raymond would have had to hide his own concepts and masquerade as an average child who saw the world like everybody else. On the other hand, Raymond's disturbance was not displayed in the raw. The sun constituted the highest level of sublimation Raymond was capable of at the time. It was almost a self-portrait projected far up into the sky, and with its smile and yellow glow it radiated warmth. The distortion of the features was reminiscent of the crooked, half-smile with which Raymond looks up to people who tower over him.

When the painting was hung in a place of honor, it demonstrated to Raymond that a person who is different can be accepted by fulfilling his potentials without having to disguise or distort his personality and without loss of identity. Naturally this feeling was the result of several years at the school where Raymond had been accepted with all his limitations, where he had learned to adjust to certain norms of behavior, and had learned to like people and to make himself liked. The painting expressed a very complex process in concentrated symbolic form. The experience had to be re-enacted after each return, because each rejection at home made it necessary to establish the feeling anew.

The fact that one of Raymond's suns was always hanging in the dining room was questioned by the children. It was explained to them that Raymond could not paint very well and that the suns were his specialty, also that seeing his sun made Raymond feel at home when he came back to us. The explanation was accepted, since each child knew that his own special requests were also fulfilled whenever possible. To Raymond, who had related better to adults, the art therapist's and the staff's acceptance of the sun was more important than his schoolmates' indifference or mild criticism. For Raymond, who had difficulties relating, the exhibition was an ideal stage whereon to act out certain problems without becoming too personally involved. The next case history is about a child who had a tremendous need to involve the whole school in his problems.

Clyde's Horror Faces

Clyde was an anxiety-ridden child of 11. He constantly provoked his schoolmates into beating him cruelly. His tortured and bruised face was a haunting sight on the campus. Later when Clyde received psychotherapeutic treatment the ups and downs of his progress could be followed by his appearance. When Clyde's face was washed and clean of scars and bruises, all was well. During setbacks he would again be dirty and bruised.

Clyde was an artistic child. He had a beautiful singing voice and sang in the choir. Also he could make up poetry, and he was a talented painter. Short of psychotherapy Clyde's most effective treatment was his singing, especially when he learned to sing solos. Here for the first time Clyde could exhibit something positive to the group.

Clyde's first paintings had the quality of nightmares. He painted innumerable fantastic faces, reminiscent of the masks of evil spirits and demons of primitive art. In spite of their horror, his paintings had much formal beauty. Clyde's paintings were a success with his schoolmates. They gave form to an anxiety which most of them also experienced to some degree.

As Clyde's fears gradually became less all-pervading, other emotions and longings were also expressed. There was a strong effort to assert himself and to master dangers. In this spirit Clyde painted many large ships sailing calmly across the ocean, also cowboys, generals, and other powerful figures. A longing for art, music, and gracious living was expressed in vivid paintings of people playing musical instruments and in domestic scenes, such as a family at dinner, etc. Clyde's moods changed so quickly that he often went through the whole gamut of emotions, from victoriously aggressive paintings to idyllic scenes, to horror pictures, in one session. At this point it was very important for Clyde to have those paintings which showed him victorious conspicuously displayed. The paintings had to be changed frequently so that his latest masterpiece would always be seen. At the same time Clyde also needed to have one of his gruesome paintings hanging in

Fig. 2. Size, 18 x 24 inches, tempera.

the dining room. The horrible face was only changed at long intervals (Fig. 2). At intervals Clyde looked through his folder, took out all horror pictures and handed them to the therapist for disposal, stating that he never wanted to see them again. But soon new horror pictures appeared. One of them had to be hung in the dining room and remained there until Clyde's next great clean-up.

In this case a child with tremendous need for dramatization and exhibitionism found a safe and constructive channel for a tendency which otherwise might have lead to great suffering and increased disturbance.

Another child whose exhibitionistic problems were helped through the dining room exhibition was Martin.

Martin, the Great Master

Martin was an all-around gifted child. He painted, sang and danced, and play-acted. His intelligence was superior. He desperately needed recognition. Besides being a seriously disturbed child, his position at the school was made more difficult because of his different cultural background. (This aspect of his problems will be discussed at great length in another context.) Martin's efforts at calling attention to his person and his accomplishments made him disliked. In the art room his pictures were frequently torn and disfigured by his exasperated schoolmates. His pictures were admired when they were exhibited in the dining room where the boys could enjoy them without being irritated by Martin's frantic bragging.

Because Martin's exhibitionism was at least partly satisfied by his success in the exhibition, he could begin to understand that bragging prevented him from gaining the recognition he deserved. He learned to control himself during art sessions and soon the others began imitating him and turning to him for help. Martin, who in his desperate quest for attention had been well on the way to making himself into the school's clown, became instead one of the recognized master painters. After his discharge he was remembered as one of Wiltwyck's great painters. His fame persisted even after the last of his former schoolmates had left Wiltwyck.

The exhibition helped each one of the three children in a different way. For Raymond it was a stage where he could act out his problem in the symbolic, detached manner which suited his personality. Clyde found an area where he could exhibit his emotions in a symbolic, sublimated form. This helped him to control his need to dramatize his problems by provoking physical punishment. Martin found a legitimate, constructive way of gratifying a strong exhibitionism and gaining the recognition and leadership he craved.

The impact of the children's experience on the group varied accordingly. Raymond's experience did not touch the other boys. Clyde involved the group in many ways. During his provocative acting out he constituted a tremendous temptation for sadistic behavior, brought out cruelty, and generated guilt. Later his horror pictures were liked and at times imitated. Martin's influence on the group was greatest. His work was admired and widely imitated. He became famous, and after his departure a legend grew around his person. Clyde and Martin were helped partly because they could assume leadership. Their leadership in turn influenced the production and development of their schoolmates. To understand the underlying dynamic process, the meaning of leadership and tradition has to be further investigated.

LEADERSHIP AND TRADITION

CHILDREN share the world of their elders only in part. They largely live in a world of their own, and their art expresses this world-within-our-world. No matter how deep his understanding and empathy for children's art may be, the adult who directs an art program cannot assume leadership in the artistic production of the children. He can help them to free themselves of influences that obstruct creative work. He can help in matters of technique and guide their growth. Certainly his personality as an artist will influence the children's work in a subtle way. Actual leadership, the emergence of styles and trends originates among the children.

The art of any larger group of children shows in miniature all the characteristic features of art at large. We see the ascendance of fashionable painters with a large crowd of imitators, the development of small schools of painting satisfying the needs of a few. We see great talents isolated because they are too far advanced to influence the group, unusual personalities who go their own ways, and so forth. We see the development of techniques and skills, growth of traditions and legends. This process of structurization forms the basis for understanding between the painters. As long as the process remains fluid it provides the optimal conditions for individual growth. When forms become too rigid freedom of expression is lost. Without any structure, communication becomes impossible. The individual is isolated and helpless and easily regresses. It is the task of the art therapist to create conditions which give both a maximum of leeway for individual expression and sufficient coherence and structure to prevent anxiety and isolation.

For the children at Wiltwyck, who distrust their own ideas and capacities, support from the group is indispensible. Just because they are basically isolated the children are afraid to stand alone. To show one's ideas without knowing whether others share them is frightening to many of the children. In such a situation it would be senseless to urge everybody to express his own ideas. Dependent children who are discouraged from following the leadership of their contemporaries will fall back on copying and tracing illustrations or give up art altogether. When children borrow ideas and techniques from each other, the interchange remains on a childlike level and can be a source of inspiration and a way of learning. Leadership easily falls into place, so that at any given moment several trends, or, schools of painting, coexist.

Our next two case histories illustrate the relationship between the child-artist and his followers. In each case the constellation is out of the ordinary, leading to unusual results, which illustrate the inner meaning of such a relationship particularly well.

Paul and John

Paul came to Wiltwyck School at 9 years of age. A straw blond boy with a fair complexion and an immobile face, he was a detached child who lived in a world of his own. He was happiest outdoors, totally fearless, and very observant of wild life. Paul came from an artist's family and was, himself, highly gifted. He painted mostly pictures of bizarre beings of his own invention. They were executed in swift, elegant brushstrokes in bright colors, without preliminary sketching. There was so much formal beauty and elegance in his creations that they were charming in spite of the weird content. In so far as the work of a disturbed ten year old can be compared with the work of a great painter, Paul's work was reminiscent of the painting of Paul Klee, the painter who created a world of his own, where the anxiety and aggression, which usually is connected with material that is far removed from

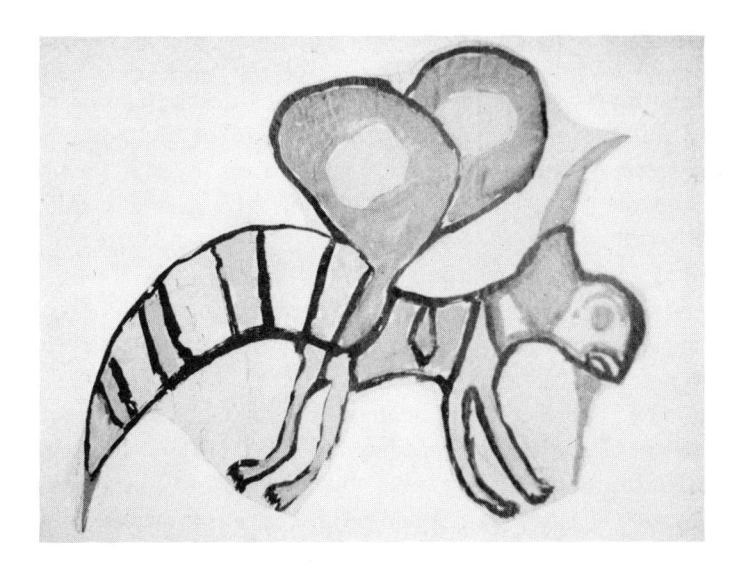

Fig. 3. Size, 18 x 24 inches, tempera.

reality, is neutralized by formal beauty, serenity, and humor. Figure 3 is a good example of Paul's style of painting.

Occasionally the boys were amused by Paul's paintings, but nobody tried to imitate him, with the exception of Martin, a very gifted and perceptive boy who somehow sensed that there was something admirable and rare in Paul's pictures. Martin tried to imitate Paul a few times, but failed totally. Paul's painting was so different from the average boy's style that nobody who did not share his state of mind could possibly imitate him. Thus Paul constituted an artist without an audience. Because he was so detached, Paul did not suffer from this lack of response.

This was the situation when John became Paul's twin and imitator. John also was a detached child who went his own ways. His early paintings had been infantile and noncommittal. Later he went through a stage during which he set very high standards of neatness and precision for himself, and became fixated to a number of stereotypes —a castle, a rainbow, and a battle at sea—which he produced over and over again, without ever being satisfied with the results.

John's relationship with Paul began with a sort of playful aggression. The boys painted pictures which made fun of each other's peculiarities and weaknesses. For example, John painted a picture of Paul with green grass for hair, because Paul had been nicknamed "Grasshead," because of his straw blond hair. Paul retaliated by painting John with his cigarette butts, because John was a compulsive smoker. During those preliminaries John's style became more infantile, freer, and quite bizarre.

Then followed a period when the two boys painted twin pictures. They worked side by side. Paul would start to paint, and, almost simultaneously, John followed him. Both boys were elated and happy. Between them they produced 10 to 15 twin pictures within a period. The pictures were almost identical. They seemed produced by two people who were literally one heart and one soul. If one compared them more closely, Paul's paintings were more intricate, more beautiful, and gayer (Fig. 4). John's pictures repeated the same figures, sim-

Fig. 4. Size, 18 x 24 inches, tempera.

Fig. 5. Size, 18 x 24 inches, tempera.

plified and clumsier (Fig. 5). The facial expressions of Paul's creatures were gay, and the whole conveyed a feeling of airy lightness. John's expressions were sad and the figures more static. John was very happy when he painted with Paul. The relationship lasted until both boys left the school.

John returned to Wiltwyck after an 8 months' absence. By this time Paul had left, and John had to paint by himself again. Repeatedly he tried to establish similar relationships with other boys, always choosing children whose work was somewhat fantastic. But he never found the gaiety and elation of his relationship with Paul with another child, and the new relationships did not last.

The paintings which John did alone were fantastic but less imaginative. *Example:* Figure 6—A ghost house with many windows; a weird face is looking out of each window, and a body without arms rises through the chimney. Strange faces in many colors are suspended in the sky above. All John's paintings depicted a world where any object, animate or inanimate, might look at you with a face. But John had trouble inventing those faces. All he knew was that he wanted a lot of ugly faces, and he often asked the teacher or a schoolmate to draw them for him. He then would use a modified version of them in his pictures. John never tried to imitate the more realistic pictures of his schoolmates, but he seemed to want to adopt the bizarre and fantastic creations of others—as if it reassured him that others also had such fantasies.

His happiest relationship of this kind had been with Paul. Here he could adopt the inner world of a child whom he resembled in many ways. Paul, too, was a detached, odd child. He, too, lived in a world of strange apparitions and removed from reality.

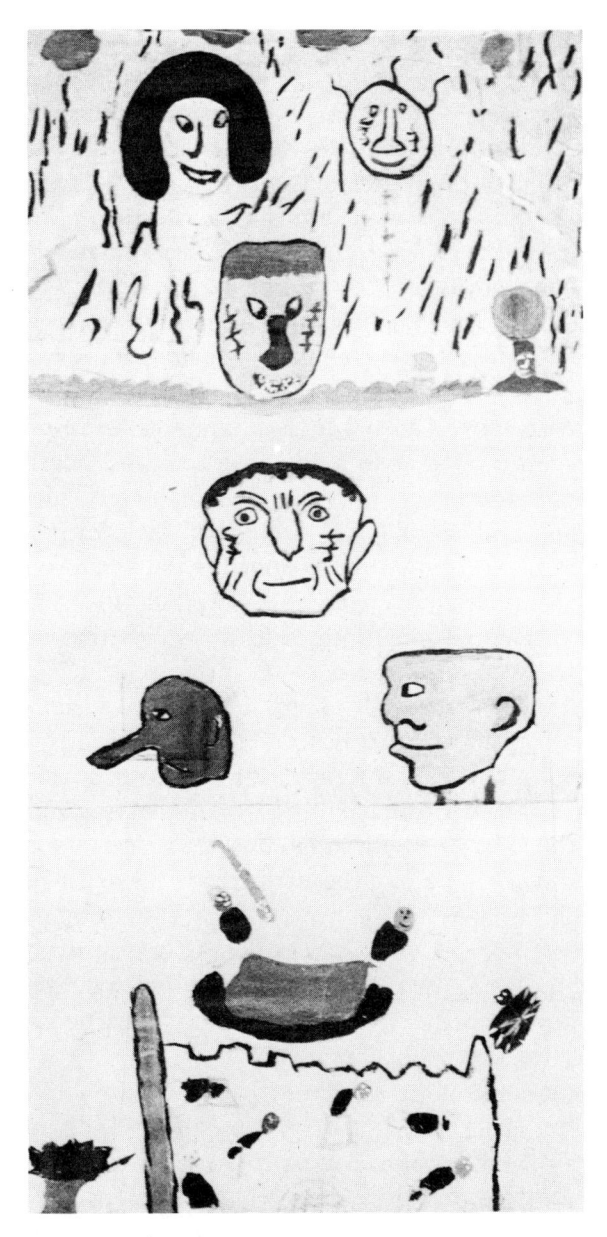

Fig. 6. Size, 24 x 54 inches, tempera.

Paul was probably the healthier child; his fantasies may have been less frightening to begin with. Certainly he was the more gifted one. His great and unusual talent made it possible for him to form and sublimate his fantasies and create pictures that were accepted by the community because they were amusing and beautiful. Paul's paintings did not mean much to his schoolmates because their inner world was too unlike Paul's world. But for the one child who was disturbed in a similar way, Paul's creations meant a great emotional gain. This gain was not achieved in the usual manner. John did not admire Paul's paintings as an adult does, nor was he inspired to create in the same style as do children who admire the paintings of other children. He completely identified with Paul, and, so to speak, exchanged his own shapeless, unformed, and frightening visions for Paul's more articulate and sublimated creations. Through this exchange John experienced something akin to sublimation. John's emotional gain seems akin to the pleasure which the enjoyment of art normally offers. Shapeless, chaotic, and frightening material is transformed into clear, articulated, visual images. But John's ego did not go through all the processes which ordinarily belong to the enjoyment of art. In the usual case the amateur's ego repeats the process of transformation along the path which the artist has laid out. Children usually express this process through copying the pictures which they admire or, more constructively, by incorporating in their own work those style elements which appeal to them. Thus the ego is enriched and its capacity for expression broadened.

John could not copy Paul's paintings after they were finished. He painted his twin pictures simultaneously with Paul, and became an artist as he was carried away by Paul's creative drive. We are reminded of a seduction, rather than of sublimation. Or of the kind of contagion which happens in group activities such as dancing, rhythm bands, or dramatic play. It was as if John's ego were too weak or too disturbed to be able to integrate and incorporate what Paul had to offer to him. Therefore, in order to enjoy Paul's art, he had to find a method more suited to his primitive and incomplete ego organization. John temporarily lost his ego and became Paul. Paul himself did not participate actively in the relationship. He enjoyed the situation but never became dependent on it.

Paul's creative process seemed complete and highly successful, but his subjects were bizarre. It seemed as though Paul's disturbance determined his subject matter and the style of his work, but that the act of creation itself was not disturbed.

Paul was an artist without an audience, not because his work was artistically inadequate, but because his unusual fantasy world did not appeal to his school mates. This lack of response was partly counterbalanced by a certain respectful appreciation for his skill and inventiveness on the part of the children, and by the art therapist's appreciation for his work. But above all, Paul's family liked his paintings, so that Paul regularly took his pictures home to a highly appreciative audience. Also Paul probably needed an audience less than the average boy, because he had very little guilt feeling and therefore no need for reassurance.

Conclusions

Paul's case shows how much the artist's success depends on a similarity of character structure between artist and public. We see the wide range of deviant fantasies and states of mind which can be formed and expressed by the gifted artist. And we see that artistic talent may coexist with severe disturbances.

In John's case we see how much the enjoyment of art depends on the amateur's capacity to integrate and incorporate what the artist has to offer. We see how the lack of such a capacity made it impossible for John to enjoy Paul's art in the usual way. But we also see how a strong need will find new and unusual ways of fulfillment when ordinary methods fail.

The next case illustrates the importance of a common cultural background for the mutual understanding between artist and audience.

Martin, the Ethiopian*

Martin and both of his parents were born in the United States. The family had originally come from Ethiopia, and the parents had perserved the Coptic religion and other cultural traditions. The family idealized Ethiopia and Ethiopian traditions against the reality of their life in New York City. When Martin came to Wiltwyck School at 10 years of age, he widely advertised his Ethiopian descent. He drew maps of Africa with Ethiopia conspicuously outlined and colored in the national colors, and he painted pictures of Ethiopian people in native dress, etc. With this he aroused a storm of anger and hostility. The Negro boys especially equated Ethiopia with Africa and considered all mention of African descent as insulting, derogatory remarks against their race and color. Martin loved to paint. Also he craved success and recognition. After an initial period of despair

---

*The reader must remember that the events described in this case occurred in the early fifties, before the advent of the civil-rights movement and the upsurge of racial pride characteristic of today's American blacks. Martin's parents were ahead of their time, and Martin had to suffer for their progressive attitude toward their African heritage.

he compromised by painting Indians instead of Ethiopians (Fig. 7).

For many Negro children painting Indians constitutes a way out of the dilemma of their minority situation.

Fig. 7. Size, 18 x 24 inches, tempera.

They hesitate to paint Negroes, but feel free to paint an Indian's skin color, and often disguise their ego ideals in the shape of Indian chiefs. But while the meaning of such a disguise is at best dimly perceived by the average Wiltwyck boy, it was for Martin a perfectly conscious disguise. He knew that he wanted to paint Ethiopians and was only bowing to necessity. There was no hypocrisy in his change of subject matter, as Martin did not lie to himself. The quality of his work therefore did not suffer from this compromise, as it probably would have suffered if Martin had denied his own ideals and superimposed an acceptance of the group's values. Eventually Martin became one of Wiltwyck's most famous and influential painters. Once his position was established he could even permit himself to paint Ethiopians. By then the boys had accepted his ideas about Ethiopia. Through the example of Haile Selassie, Martin even created a vogue for painting Negro kings, which had tremendous effect on the self-esteem of Wiltwyck's Negro population.

Eventually Martin's own feelings about Ethiopia changed. He did not give up his ideals, but he accepted the reality of his life in the United States and had less need to idealize a past of which he had no personal knowledge. His need to use art for idealizing the Negro remained, but he now painted American Negroes, idealizing them in a realistic manner, such as a glamorous Negro singer in evening dress before a microphone. Later he painted his mother and thus established the realistic acceptance of his race and color and ancestry (Plate I colorprint).

Freed from his singleminded preoccupation, his subject matter became more varied, so that he was the originator of many fashions and fads in the school. Upon his discharge he drew one last picture on the train to New

York (Fig. 8). It depicted his street, with himself on the rooftop flying a kite. He had accepted the reality of his life in the city.

Conclusions

Martin's story shows an artist's work being rejected because of his cultural background. The artist chooses a subject matter which touches upon prejudices in a group. A negative emotional reaction to the subject matter makes the audience blind to the artistic value of his work.

Fig. 8. Size, 6 x 8 inches, pencil.

Historically such situations occur frequently when two cultures mingle. There usually is an initial period of mutual misunderstanding and disorientation, and consequently a decline of the arts. The ultimate outcome depends on the relative cultural and economic strength of the two groups, on the degree to which their two moral codes are at variance, on a time factor and other conditions.

It might happen that a people who conquers a culturally strong group by military power, adopts the culture of the conquered people, as it happened when Ancient Greece was incorporated into the Roman Empire. It also happened repeatedly in Chinese history when nomadic conquerors were habitually conquered by Chinese culture and tradition. But this is possible only when the conquered people can preserve their integrity as a cultural group and when the moral code remains intact.

Whenever the new order of things absolutely contradicts the old moral code, the old art forms will perish. We can observe such a decline often when a native culture is overrun by industrialism.

In so far as one can compare an individual case with historical events, we might say that Martin constituted a culturally strong minority within a group who conquered this group by the strength of his talent, his intelligence, and the power of his convictions. This could not have happened if Martin had given up his convictions instead of expressing them in disguise. If Martin had capitulated before group pressure, he would have lost his past, his ideals and his integrity as an individual. His creative capacity would probably not have survived such a loss. If, on the other hand, Martin had insisted on his convictions with a martyr's zeal, and had survived physically, his style and subject matter would probably have become stereotyped and repetitious. He would have remained isolated, and it would have become very difficult for him to develop as a person and as an artist.

In spite of his talent and intelligence, Martin could not have survived the initial period of his adjustment unaided. The device to hide the meaning of his paintings under the disguise of Indians was of his own choice, but he could not have maintained it without sharing the secret with the art therapist. Nor could Martin and his schoolmates have resolved their ideological conflicts without adults who helped to clarify the true relationship between Ethiopia, Africa, and the American Negro. The therapeutic aim was to help the child to adjust as an artist and as an individual in the group, without robbing him of his cultural heritage, and to make the positive values which Martin had to offer become a part of the cultural life of the group.

KINGS, PRISONERS, AND MONSTERS

The rise and decline of styles and its meaning for the individual is too complex to be presented in full. The three major trends which are described here center around emotions connected with self-esteem, delinquency, and anxiety and aggression.

KINGS

Of all new subjects which Martin had introduced at the school, his Negro kings made the most lasting impression. For Martin himself the painting of Negro kings was an episode which he soon outgrew.

The fashion of the Kings was perpetuated by Carl. Carl was an American Negro. He was talented, though less gifted and not as intelligent as Martin. Temperamentally he was Martin's opposite. He painted slowly, with much attention to detail. His colors were muted and soft. His painting seemed set in a minor key. Carl was tremendously attracted to Martin. He imitated him and competed with him. When Martin was discharged, Carl, as the next best painter, inherited Martin's position. Even then he continued measuring himself against Martin. Carl was a child who expected failure. Many of his paintings showed a hero who is being slain. For instance: a rider who is being shot in the back by an Indian arrow; two sword fighters, one of them stabbed in the breast, his sword dropping to the ground; two knights at arms, one of them lying dead. In all the pictures the loser is painted with great care and occupies the center of the painting.

The killer is masked, hidden, or encased in armor. Carl is clearly identified with the loser.

Carl had much reason to have a tragic sense of life. His father was a delinquent who was seldom out of prison. The family existed on the verge of destitution with little hope for change. Carl's longing for ideals and cultural values could not find fulfillment at home. He felt menaced by his father's violence and the brutalized home situation which evoked his own dormant aggression. He lived under a cloud of depression. Because of his personal history, problems of racial discrimination became highly charged emotionally. Beneath the question whether Negroes could assume leading positions loomed the question whether he, as his father's son, could rise above him. The desire to be re-born white screened the desire to be rid of the delinquent father and with it to be rid of his own delinquent tendencies.

When Carl took over Martin's Negro Kings, their image became charged with Carl's conflicts, and, what had been an episode for Martin, become for Carl a major preoccupation. Carl perfected the Kings, gave them, so to speak, their final iconic form. Figure 9 shows one of Carl's most beautiful Kings. It is quite a self-portrait, a fine-featured melancholic man who carries his honors with quiet dignity. The monocle in his right eye gives a strange asymetry to the face, as if some part of the personality remained ambiguous. The picture is painted on grey paper. Except for the yellow golden jewelry all colors are subdued. Dark blue, dark purple, a little red, and a spot of bright green at the open collar, brown fur inside the collar, give a dignified over-all effect. Space is handled beautifully; the straight line of the scepter gives balance and interest to the composition. The painting fulfilled Carl's need for beauty, dignity, and success.

Fig. 9. Size, 24 x 36 inches, tempera.

Yet there is no exuberance in the work. It is fulfillment within the limitation of a basic depression and deep resignation.

Carl's imitators closely followed the pattern which he had established. Although choice of color and arrangement of ornament and shade of skin color varied, the basic form remained unaltered. Among the innumerable Kings that were painted at this period, there was not one who did not wear the same type of crown, not one without monocle in his right eye. It would have been impossible to induce a child to paint a monocle-less king. He would have seemed incomplete. (There was among the many Kings only one with monocle in the left eye, he had been painted by a left-handed child.)

Carl had taken the monocle from comic books, where they are worn by rich men. Originally he had used it in a painting of a white man in evening dress. From there he carried it over to the Kings. To Carl the monocle had probably unconscious significance. It might have symbolized the split between good and bad, and the shady hidden side of his character. Some of the symbolic meaning might have carried over to the others. But the persistency of the monocle is above all a phenomena of group behavior. We are observing how tradition is formed and perpetuated.

At the beginning there had been Martin, a strong original mind, who had painted the first King. To him it was meaningful for a time, then he outgrew it. The idea was picked up by Carl, who found a way of expressing his personal conflict within the form which Martin had originated. Carl's ambivalence around problems of race and success was too great to find expression independently. He needed somebody else's example to give him courage. Because of the deep emotional significance of the subject

Carl elaborated on it and evolved a simple and impressive form. Because the problem persisted, Carl periodically painted replicas of the King. As the painting was cast in its final form, it was adopted by the multitude and perpetuated without further changes. Every detail from then on was an attribute of the symbol King, and only a very strong and independent mind would have questioned any detail or attempted to alter it. Because of the fast turnover in population the form was preserved, not for a century, but for 2 years only.

Among the children the symbol of the King continued to serve as a means of expressing problems of self-esteem and self-evaluation. The license to paint Negro Kings persisted. Carl's need for culture and beauty also was retained in a subtle way. As an object of identification the King remained on a higher, more civilized emotional level than, for instance, the Indian chieftain. A king carries a scepter—not a raised tomahawk. His crown is the work of complex craftsmanship, unlike the chieftain's headgear which retains the character of a trophy. Indeed the children who chose to paint Kings were as a rule more mature emotionally, and, in turn, the painting of Kings had a civilizing influence on the children. Therapeutically the King had been valuable at first for Martin, later for Carl, and in the final analysis for the whole community. However, traditions cannot be perpetuated beyond their natural life. Eventually the painting of Kings went out of fashion.

The rise and fall of ideas and tradition cannot be regulated from outside. The meeting of two personalities like Martin and Carl is a happy coincidence which cannot be brought about artificially. Even if the art therapist could have guessed intuitively that Carl need to paint Negro Kings, the therapist's suggestion would never have carried the weight of an admired schoolmate's living example. For working the problem through the participation of the group was essential.

The art therapist's function was to recognize the emotional significance of the development, and to see to it that it did not break down. For instance, the painting of dark skin colors needed support from the therapist. Again and again her help was needed in the mixing of various shades of brown, and again and again it had to be demonstrated to the children that all shades of skin contain much the same colors in different proportions, more white for white people, more brown for Negroes, etc. Both lack of support or over-insistence on the problem of painting Negro skins might have ended the painting of Kings.

The art therapist's actions and attitudes were geared to conveying to the children the feeling that the unconscious meaning of their efforts was understood and accepted, without bringing more of the problem to consciousness than they could tolerate.

PRISONERS

The next example is the history of an episode which lasted barely three weeks and involved just a small group of boys. The originator of the fashion of painting prisoners was Jerry. At the time of the episode Jerry was recognized as one of Wiltwyck's ablest painters. He had a great need for display. From the beginning he affected a somewhat theatrical, blustering he-man attitude. Strutting about with thrust-out chest, clenched fists, and an exaggerated frown, he also developed a peculiar abrupt and blurred kind of speech. His mannerisms were dear to him. He was immune against criticism or ridicule from adults and succeeded in making his schoolmates admire and imitate his ways. In spite of his tough act, Jerry was no serious discipline problem. He was impulsive, but not destructive, and was as a rule open to reason.

Jerrys' behavior was reminiscent of the stereotyped picture of a volcano which he used to paint when he first came to the school. His volcano, a conical grey mountain on a tropical island with palm trees showed an eruption of red flames topped by a thick black cloud. No destruction was visible, and the volcanic mood did not pervade the rest of the landscape, which was peaceful and pretty. Jerry's volcano erupted for display rather than for destruction, just as Jerry's tough behavior seemed to be motivated by a need for narcissictic gratification rather than by hostility. Jerry did not limit himself to volcanoes for long. Soon his subject matter covered most of the interests. of the "regular boy." He painted cowboys, Spaniards, sword fighters, rich men and evening clothes, pirates, and gangsters. In accordance with his need for display he became expert at painting fancy clothes and accessories such as plumed hats, ornate weapons, walking sticks, buttons, and buckles. His interest was shared by the group, and his ability added to his prestige.

Jerry's painting had much formal beauty. His sense of color was exquisite. He preferred cool colors, using small areas of warm color for effect within preponderantly cool compositions. His work had action, interest, and clarity. His paintings were not expressive emotionally. Even when his subject matter was dramatic, neither his people's expressions nor the formal element of the painting conveyed strong feelings. Jerry's relationship to his own talent remained guarded. He did not permit himself to get too deeply involved with art. His relationship to the art therapist was amiable but impersonal. His painting seldom revealed deeper feelings and conflicts. It was probably the combination of a strong narcissism and the cold impersonal quality of his work that made Jerry into a fashionable painter who was widely imitated. His schoolmates never considered Jerry a top painter. The boys who were considered master painters all had not only talent, but also a great passion for art. Their work had depth and scope that went beyond the average child's reach. Although they were imitated, there remained a certain distance between them and the rest of the group.

Jerry was closer to the group. His work embodied the group ideal without going beyond it. Jerry did not try to compete with the top painters. He seemed content with the narcissistic satisfaction of seeing himself reflected in the work of his followers and imitators. As a type Jerry may be compared to a painter like Van Dyke. A superb craftsman who combined sensitivity as a portraitist with virtuosity at painting the paraphernalia of wealth and satisfied his clientele without going beyond their needs and expectations, an admirable painter whose work never reached the scope of a Rubens, the vitality of a Franz Hals, or Rembrandt's depth.

Jerry was the first to paint a prisoner (Fig. 10). Although gangsters and hold-up men, or scenes of romantic escapes from medieval castles, or dungeons were painted frequently, nobody had painted a modern prisoner before. To delinquent children who live in a delinquent environment, prison is a serious menace. The subject is therefore usually avoided.

Jerry's prisoner (Fig. 10) is shackled and guarded. Behind him rises the grey stone wall which symbolizes his confinement. The prisoner's person dominates the painting. Guards and fellow prisoners are dwarfed. His position is that of a man waiting. There is a certain nonchalance in his posture. His facial expression is calm, almost deadpan. With his usual taste for clothes, Jerry

Fig. 10. Size, 24 x 36 inches, tempera.

has transformed the prisoner's uniform into a costume, using the black and white stripes to their most decorative advantage. Even the number tag seems an ornament. The formal composition is beautifully balanced. The combination of grey and black and a brilliant white have a calm, almost abstract beauty. The warm flesh color of the prisoner's face and hands and a few spots of warm brown give life and interest to the composition. The prisoner is protected by a calm, nonchalant attitude and by his elegant beauty. He is superior to his situation, and has no need to rebel, or to repent. Jerry's position as a leader of fashions in painting, along with the example of a painting of a prisoner which did not arouse anxiety, encouraged a number of boys to follow his example.

Walter's painting (Plate II colorprint) expresses all the emotions which Jerry's avoids. Some of the characteristics of Jerry's composition are preserved. The prisoner also holds the center of the stage. He is large, almost life size, while his fellow prisoners and the guard are tiny figures. The resemblance ends here. Walter's background is a deep black. The ground is painted in wild red brushstrokes. The black stripes of the prisoner's suit merge with the background and convey the feeling that the prisoner emerges out of darkness and belongs to darkness. The horizontal lines which traverse his body give the impression that the prisoner is eradicated by black lines. The fact that the prisoner's limbs are only partly visible (feet and hands are outside the picture) conveys a feeling of helplessness, almost mutilation. The face is expressive; a broad, tightly-closed mouth contrasts with small, weak eyes.

Walter had much reason to feel strongly about prisoners. His father was serving a sentence and had been in and out of jails all of Walter's life. Walter did not admit this. He told boastful tales about his father's wealth and power.

Plate II represents Walter's second version of a prisoner. He had first attempted to paint a prisoner with raised pickax ready to split a rock. This painting was bound to be a failure. Walter was upset at the start, demanded excessive support from the therapist and remained dissatisfied and querulous. Eventually he went into a tantrum, wherein he had to be prevented from tearing up every picture in his folder and wrecking the art room. A week later Walter very quietly painted his prisoner (Plate II colorprint) without any help.

Emotionally Walter was in every way Jerry's opposite. Just as Jerry had expressed his personality in his first stereotyped picture of a volcano, Walter's temperament found expression first in a picture of a boat, of which he painted several versions. It was a large black and white and red motor boat at sea, silhouetted against a huge rising sun in orange and a pink sky. The painting had the exuberance and violent emotionality which characterized Walter and his work. His later subject matter was extremely varied. He painted heroes, both good and bad, sailors and pirates, robbers and angels, hold-up men and generals, also scenes of violence and adventure, and idyllic pictures of women with flowers, landscapes, etc. Walter commanded a tremendous range of moods. His capacity for expressing his feelings through creative work was an aid in his struggle to maintain a precarious emotional balance.

Jerry's prisoner gave Walter the courage to find expression for feeling about his father, which he would not put into words since overtly he denied his father's incarceration. During his first attempt Walter was overwhelmed by his murderous feelings. Although the prisoner's raised pickax was rationalized as a gesture of splitting a rock, the rationalization insufficiently screened murderous violence. Walter's inability to complete the painting seemed a sign of health. This is borne out by the transformation which took place in Walter's second, successful painting (Plate II). Here feelings are internalized. The prisoner's hands and feet are out of the picture; action and mobility are inhibited. Although the red ground expresses violence, the dominant color is black, the dominant motions are horizontals, and the prisoner's face is sad. Facts are accepted, violence is controlled, and the dominant feelings are of depression and despair.

Fletcher was another child who was inspired by Jerry's prisoner. He painted a bird's eye view of the prison and its fortifications. Prisoners were at work breaking stones, loading them into pushcarts, and carting them off. Fletcher was an habitual runaway, who pilfered and committed acts of vandalism. His salvation was his love of constructive work. He was an excellent carpenter and builder. His clear logical mind, manual skill, and passion for work made him the school's master craftsman. Feltcher described his addiction to work in these words: "Other boys try to get out of work; I am a boy who tries to get into work." Fletcher had no ability to play; idleness inevitably led to delinquent acts.

In his painting Fletcher depicted the one thing which could make prison life bearable to him: hard labor. Fletcher had good reasons to be concerned with the life of prisoners. In spite of an understanding of right and wrong, in spite of talent for leadership and constructive work, his tendency for asocial acts persisted. Fletcher could easily end up in prison, and there he would certainly survive only if he were given enough work.

Fig. 11. Size, 24 x 36 inches, tempera.

Bernard depicted the prisoner as a monster (Fig. 11). Against a deep red background looms head and long torso of a prisoner. His long arms reach to the bottom of the page. The hands are out of the picture. The prisoner's face is without mouth and nose. His right eye is almost covered by a large scar. The left eye is square and placed in the middle of the forehead. Another large scar traverses the prisoner's left cheek. The painting has the character of an apparition from a nightmare. The painting expresses neither anxiety nor guilt or rebellion. It expresses a feeling of depersonalization and incompleteness. The prisoner is beyond human empathy or moral code.

Bernard came to Wiltwyck when he was barely 10. He was undersized and sexually underdeveloped. With his blond hair, blue eyes, and rosy complexion he looked like a little doll. Bernard was an expert thief, specializing in picking ladies' pocketbooks and lifting wrist watches. He did not wish to grow up, but planned to remain small and cute and live by theft. Even after he had ceased stealing, Bernard took pride in his skills. One of his favorite jokes consisted of lifting a wrist watch without the owner's notice and then innocently asking for the time.

The prisoner painting shows Bernard's deep feeling of estrangement from mankind. Successful stealing is equated with proof of potency and completeness, and failure with multilation and loss of face. In Bernard's prisoner no attempt is made at working through the guilt and anxiety of delinquency. Rather it shows the terrible results of being unsuccessful.

Discussion

Among the children who painted pictures of prisoners, Jerry was the only one who found a solution for the fears and conflicts which were attached to the idea. Jerry's equilibrium was based on a kind of withdrawal into narcissism and emotional shallowness. Jerry's example encouraged his schoolmates to tackle a subject which they had reasons to avoid. For Jerry himself, the prisoner may have been a preparation for a series of paintings which had greater emotional depth. Soon after the prisoner painting, Jerry depicted the outbreak and control of a forest fire in a series of pictures. In this series the problem of impulse control was dramatized with great emotional intensity.

Walter's prisoner constituted a first step in coming to grips with a fact which he would have to face eventually. Although the painting did not mean a full admittance of reality, it constituted an attempt at sounding out the many contradictory feelings centered around the fathers' person. Between the first painting and the completed version there is a change from overt murderous violence towards violence subdued by depression, a state of mind which easily can revert to actual hostility. The two paintings are a typical example of Walter's emotional swings which made the integration of his emotional gains so very difficult and precarious. In the particular case of the prisoners, though, not much more could be expected even of a less disturbed child. Walter had to come to terms with a situation for which no 11 year old child is equipped. No resolution of the conflict could be hoped for at the time.

Fletcher reassured himself by depicting the one aspect of prison life which he could possibly accept. The painting expresses the single-mindedness which had been Fletcher's salvation in the past but threatened to become a danger in the future. In his future life Fletcher would have to submit to periods of idleness and boredom at school, and later as a working man. Up-to-date he had failed to develop methods of coping with the panic and hostility such situations aroused in him. Conceivably the painting even expressed the hidden desire for the security of the rigid discipline of prison life. To the observer the painting confirmed what was apparent in the child's general behavior—that Fletcher was suppressing his emotional problems by an obsessive concentration on work. There remained the need to help the child to work those problems through in order to make an adjustment which would admit of other pleasures and experiences besides building and carpentry.

Bernard's painting showed very graphically that underneath his cute exterior and his superficial adjustment there remained a feeling of depersonalization and incompleteness which life at the school had not altered.

The episode of the prisoners was brief. We see how each child came up against problems and feelings for which there was neither solution nor reconciliation within his reach. It is therefore not surprising that the subject was dropped after a time. The experience remained valuable, because many problems were brought to the surface although they could not be resolved beyond a certain point. Because the prisoner was not a symbol which means more or less the same to everyone, as does a king, but was part of reality with different meanings for each individual, no rigid form for painting prisoners evolved.

MONSTERS

It is to be expected that part of the production of disturbed children should be given over to bizarre and fantastic subjects and that evil and uncanny themes should play an important part in those productions. Devils, dragons, giants, ghosts, and monsters, and the fabulous creatures of science fiction, embody the forces of evil for the children. Murderous and monstrous animals such as sharks, snakes, and octopuses often take on the same meaning.

The painting of monsters constitutes only a minor part of the total production in the group. Paintings of heroes, such as Indians, cowboys, kings, etc., and horses, boats, airplanes, and other reassuring symbols of power and potency prevail over monsters and fabulous creatures. It is interesting that occasions such as Hallowe'en, which seem to invite the painting of fantastic subjects, do not alter the balance between the two trends. The license to paint witches, ghosts, and other monsters is taken up only by children who are inclined to paint them anyway. Or rather, only those children's monsters carry conviction. Children who have no inner need for painting them produce tame stereotypes which convey no emotion.

Even a latent need for the expression of monstrous fantasies is seldom freed by an outside occasion. Latent fantasies are brought out mostly through stimulation within the group. And here again leadership becomes important.

It would be a mistake to believe that the painting of fantastic subjects would be free of convention and stereotypes. Most of the children are just as helpless if confronted with the idea of having to invent a Marsman or a dragon as they would be in the face of more realistic subject matter. The suggestion that there is no such thing as a Marsman or a dragon and that therefore anything they might invent would be all right, has no meaning. There exist definite stereotypes for the representation of Marsmen, devils, even monster faces, which have to be adhered to, and here, as everywhere, deviation from the norm arouses anxiety.

As a rule, only very withdrawn and detached children or very creative children are free from those limitations.

Because every child experiences his share of fears and nightmares, the production of most gifted children contains some monsters. They bear witness to the child's creative scope, which gives form to a multitude of diverse feelings and experiences. It is interesting that Jerry, Wiltwyck's fashionable painter, was one of the few gifted children who never painted a monster, probably because of his general reluctance to disclose his private feelings. Leadership rests with those children whose production is predominately given to fantastic and imaginative painting and who have the talent to create new forms and ideas. Paintings of this kind are not very numerous and examples of leadership are limited to small groups only.

The reader has been acquainted in this book with three painters of monsters and fantastic subjects: Paul and John and Clyde. (Bernard's prisoner belongs to the same order but was not characteristic of his general production.)

Paul and Clyde

Paul's style was described briefly in the section on Leadership and Tradition (Paul and John, Figs. 3, 4, 5 and 6). Paul created a world of his own, populated by fantastic creatures of his invention. In creating this world, Paul bypassed the monstrous and gruesome with the ease and grace of a tightrope walker. Not that aggression was absent in his work. (His bee—Fig. 3—has three stingers; her pink back ending in a sharp red stinger could hardly be more symbolic or more aggressive.) But Paul's treatment gives the subject a fanciful lightness and irresponsibility which bypasses associations of cruelty and pain and leaves no feeling of guilt and anxiety. Paul's great talent, his unerring sense of balance and color, permitted the expression of fantasies that would have reverted under a heavier touch to unmitigated crude and bizarre symbolism.

Indeed, Paul's earliest work had been cruder, more monstrous, and, at times, very cruel. Always there had been an absence of feelings of guilt or of moral values. His preference for bizarre, fantastic painting never changed, and Paul's basic personality remained the same until his discharge. But probably because no excessive demands for performance and emotional response were made and because his individuality had been accepted, Paul's withdrawal became less stubborn and less hostile as time went on. Cruelty and monstrosity receded or were transformed through the increasing elegance and subtlety of his painting.

It was described previously how Paul's work left the majority of the children cold and that later John became Paul's alter ego and twin. The only other child to be attracted to Paul's painting was Clyde. (Clyde's horror faces (Fig. 2) were described in the section on Leadership and Tradition.) Temperamentally the two children were opposites. Clyde was given to tremendous emotional swings, he was racked with anxiety and guilt, and in constant need of emotional response. Paul was detached, absolutely fearless, and his sense of good and evil was not properly developed. Both children painted fantastic pictures, and were not much touched by conventional subject matter.

When Clyde's mother died after a long illness, he went through an episode during which painting became almost impossible for him; he helped himself by borrowing Paul's ideas and working close to him. Paul was one of the few children who was rarely provoked by Clyde's ways. Unless Clyde physically interfered with his painting, Paul was tolerant of Clyde's nervousness, incessant talking and singing, and other expressions of anxiety.

As Clyde took over Paul's subject matter, he brought out the monstrosity and anxiety which had been neutralized in Paul's treatment. As a rule Clyde's versions had greater emotional depth; Paul's originals had grace and elegance beyond Clyde's reach. Clyde's painting was more human; Paul's work, more artistic. The difference corresponds to the difference in the two children's character and disturbances.

Clyde used Paul's painting and personality as a steadying influence at a time of great inner turmoil. He could not have found support by imitating a more conventional painter because such painting would not have corresponded to his inner needs. Paul's painting, even though it had different emotional content, could be transformed to express Clyde's feelings. When his emotional difficulties lessened, Clyde lost his dependency on Paul.

Paul's painting had served as a support for two schoolmates, Clyde and John, who needed a fearless and gifted leader to explore and give form to irrational and bizarre feelings and ideas that ordinarily remain hidden and chaotic.

Clyde

Clyde's painting and personality were closer to the group. His paintings embodied feelings and fears which were shared by many of his schoolmates. His earliest horror faces were painted under tremendous pressure, execution was rapid and often incoherent. Clyde's painting of this period was not imitated by his schoolmates.

Figure 2 was painted at a later date when horror pictures were no longer Clyde's only subject matter. At this time Clyde had reached a certain measure of control over his problems, and with it his painting had become clearer and more intelligible. Figure 2 expresses the very essence of fear of the dark: a rectangular sheet of paper is covered with black. Upon this surface appears a pair of large, round white eyes surrounded by short yellow-white rays. Two parallel rows of brushstrokes suggest teeth and mouth; other lines and dots combine to form nose, eyebrows, and two angry lines on either side of the mouth, all in white.

The features do not seem to be part of a solid head. They seem to float upon the dark, forming a face but ready to change into different configurations or to disappear at any instant like an hallucination or a bad dream.

The treatment of single features as separate units is chracteristic of paintings and sculptures of the miraculous and irrational throughout the ages. Especially in the masks of primitives organs such as eyes, nose, and mouth are often charged with individual symbolic meaning, so that the mask does not represent the unity of a face, but rather a stage on which the dramatic interplay between the several features is enacted. Distortions and displacements can be understood as expressions of this drama.

It is also interesting that white drawings on black almost always express a precarious balance between the rational and irrational. The effort to impose form upon a black surface necessarily remains an unequal struggle in which the formless and hidden prevails over the visible and rational. Examples of these tendencies can be found in the graphic work of Odilion Redon, where white on black is used extensively, or earlier in the work of the German draftsman Albrecht Altdofer and many others.

Clyde's painting was a great success with his schoolmates. It was impressive and it was easy to copy. Children with a need to express the dark side of life adopted the form and contributed variations. It is interesting that, once the form is found, the painting of nightmares often has a positive effect on the painter's mood. Habitually depressed or belligerent children become amiable and cooperative while painting their monsters. This indicates that their painting means more than just release for their feelings. It shows that through painting the children obtain temporary mastery over their conflicts so that the burden of anxiety and aggression is eased for them.

Harry, Master of Monsters

Harry came to the school at the age of 11. He was an overweight boy, withdrawn, polite, and anxious to please. He was intelligent and an avid reader. Often he seemed lost in daydreams, sitting quietly sucking his thumb. Within his first year he lost all excess weight, became slim and agile, and began participating in activities. He read out loud to his schoolmates and told fantastic stories of his own invention and was liked and admired for his gift. His daydreaming and thumbsucking persisted. Harry liked painting from the beginning. He worked quietly, with great absorption, and undisturbed by any amount of turmoil around him. Most of his painting was given over to illustrations of tales he had read and fantasies he had woven around them. Like Paul, Harry had a way of giving even commonplace subjects an out-of-this world touch. Even a Santa Claus by Harry, complete with all conventional attributes, would somehow take on an indefinable quality of belonging to another, private world.

The emotional and moral content of Harry's painting ranged from religious themes, through charming fairy tales, to tales of violence, fiendish cruelty and horror. Harry's treatment was alike for all subjects. He invariably outlined all figures and objects with a strong, even black line, and filled them in with solid color. Backgrounds were left white, or colored slightly with loose brushstrokes, or sometimes the background was strewn with crosshatching like tick-tac-toe signs, which added to the decorative effect.

Harry's bright colors and black outlines recall peasant art, especially decorations on pottery. The method is simple and effective. Any color gains strength and brilliance when surrounded with black, and almost any color combination remains harmonious. As an element of a painting the black outline constitutes at once a harmonizing and an isolating factor. The black creates harmony since it is the all-pervading element of the picture. At the same time it prevents blending and fusion of color and shapes as each area remains separate. This limits expressiveness, since volume, depth, and space cannot be fully realized. Everything appears to be on a single plane; subtle transitions and complex relationships cannot be expressed. Unity is created by the combination of parts into decorative patterns, not through their fusion into an organic whole. Within the limitations of his style Harry's painting was expressive. Action was vividly depicted. Black outlines prevailed even in scenes of violence and fast motion. In battle scenes, gunfire, explosions, and blood were carefully placed and neatly outlined.

Harry's feeling about his work seemed innocent of moral values. Just as he used the same technique for Santa Claus or a monster, he valued both paintings equally. He had a way of giving his most gruesome pictures as presents to beloved adults with the best intentions of pleasing them. It was a great victory when Harry presented the school's nurse with a painting of a fairy flying in a pink sky, because he realized that the subject would appeal to a middle-aged, kind-hearted woman.

Harry's painting revealed a mind both fantastic and bizarre, and logical and precise. His logical mind shows clearest in a series of three instruments of execution: an executioner's block and ax, a gallows, and a guillotine (Fig. 12). Each painting shows the instrument of murder silhouetted against a light sky. No victim is visible, the execution is over, and only a few drops of blood on the blade of the ax and block and on the blade of the guillotine tell the story. The gallows picture shows a grave in the background. The three paintings are beautifully composed. Especially the guillotine, with its clear, functional drawing of the mechanism, achieves a somber sort of beauty which does not detract from the cold, menacing cruelty of the painting. Behind the painting one feels a clear, methodical mind at work that has considered all details of the operation thoroughly. The paintings were much admired. A few children tried imitating the guillotine, but none of the boys of the same cruel bent had the mechanical understanding necessary for drawing the machine.

A few weeks later Harry attained fame and leadership through a series of monster heads. The first and most important of the heads was inspired by Hans Christian Anderson's fairy tale, *The Traveling Companion*. In this story a wicked princess has a gigantic monster for a lover. In the end the giant is beheaded and the head shown to the princess. On a huge sheet of brown wrapping paper Harry painted a dead-white, bald head, with several gold and silver horns protruding from the skull. Two eyes were green, and there was a third red eye in the middle of the forehead. The monster has yellow lips and teeth, and the cavity of the mouth is black. The nose is a complicated form with two large curled nostrils and gives almost the impression of a head-within-a-head. Black lines

90   *Art Therapy in a Children's Community*

Fig. 12.   Size, 18 x 24 inches, tempera.

around mouth and eyes add expression to the face. Everything is neatly outlined in black. The background is

Fig. 13. Size, 30 x 40 inches, tempera.

painted in loose red brushstrokes. In spite of its monstrosity and cruelty the painting possessed a bizarre kind of beauty. Harry was inordinately proud of his masterpiece, and could not wait to have it exhibited in the dining room.

Fig. 14. Size, 24 x 36 inches, tempera.

After admiring the painting duly, the art therapist, in an attempt to ascertain whether Harry had any idea that the painting was gruesome, suggested that it should be taken off the dining room wall for Easter when parents and baby brothers and sisters would be visiting, because some of the little children might be frightened by the monster. Harry seemed taken aback. He evidently did not conceive of his painting as frightening. (Easter was still months away, so that his reaction was not biased by the fear that his painting would be taken down too soon.)

Harry's monster created a sensation. Since Paul and Clyde's discharges 2 years ago there had been no important painter of the bizarre and fantastic at the school. Seeing a schoolmate give clear and bold form to ideas which usually remain buried evoked a shocked kind of admiration from the group. It inspired a number of children to follow suit. Monster painting became fashionable. It never took on a rigid form comparable to the fashion in Kings; nor was the trend as widespread or as lasting.

Unfortunately Harry took his monster home, so that the reader can see his work only by reflection in the paintings of his followers. Matthew (Fig. 14) and Edgar (Plate III). None of the paintings has its model's power and precision. Figure 13 was the last monster Harry painted. It is included mainly as the only available example of Harry's style. The painting constitutes the end of a development. The symbolism is here so involved and private that it no longer served as a model for his schoolmates.

Matthew

Matthew had come to Wiltwyck about a year before the monster episode. He was then 10½ years old. He suffered from a permanent sort of diarrhea that led to frequent soiling. The symptom had persisted through Matthew's childhood and seemed to be psychosomatic.

There were reasons to believe that the symptoms had been kept alive more by a need in the child's mother than by the boy's own disturbance. Upon separation from the mother Matthew's soiling and diarrhea disappeared gradually without aid of individual psychotherapy beyond treatment sessions with the social worker.

Matthew's earliest painting was decorative and noncommital. He decorated boxes and baskets or made designs. His color was bright, clear, and varied. As his soiling diminished Matthew's style changed. He ceased painting designs and began making minute drawings of fish and weapons, carefully shaded with pencil. The drawings showed intelligence, skill, and a strong sense of composition. Later Matthew tried painting larger pictures of the fish and weapons he had drawn so well. He seemed to be reaching out for greater scope and freedom, but somehow was paralyzed. Whenever Matthew used color he soon grew dissatisfied and impatient and ended by smearing and splashing paint, until his drawing was obliterated. Often Matthew tried to redeem the mess by adding more color, creating a kind of Rorschach design by folding and reopening the paper. While this consoled him a little, it naturally did not satisfy him. Things reached a point where Matthew predicted disaster the minute he touched a paint brush. Even so, Matthew continued to come to art sessions although he spent most of his time standing around unhappily.

At this point Harry painted his monster. Matthew immediately set out to paint a monster, too (Fig. 14). He was in high spirits, worked without hesitation, and used color freely. Altogether Matthew painted three monsters in quick succession, and after this he painted a fantastic castle of his own invention. This ended the episode and Matthew went back to realistic painting.

During the episode a change had taken place. Matthew was now able to use color. He painted a three-masted sailboat on a bright blue sea, its sails swelling in the breeze and waves going high in a steady rhythm (Fig. 15). There were shadings and variations of color but no muddy color. The painting showed Matthew's sense for the dec-

Fig. 15. Size, 18 x 24 inches, tempera.

orative combined with a new clarity and security in form and movement. From then on Matthew continued to paint and draw freely. He painted a series of weapons (arranged in decorative patterns, for display rather than use). Later he went around the campus with a sketchbook which he filled with drawings of trees, buildings, and animals. The difficulties around color persisted to a degree. There still were incidents of smearing, but the problem was now accessible to treatment.

Matthew's monster (Fig. 14) loses much through reproduction in black and white. The monster's face is painted in three colors. The skull is a light olive green, below the eyes runs a strip of lighter green, and the lower part of the face is painted a kind of mustard color. The right eye is black with a red iris, the left eye red. The nose, which looks somewhat like a cow's head, is dark brown and orange. The strange designs below are yellow, purple, and orange. The lips are red, teeth white, cavity of the mouth the brown wrapping paper, and the third eye below the mouth is blue with red iris. Behind the head is some sort of weapon with a black handle and red-brown blade. The monster's expression is pained and cruel. The red lips and sharp gleaming teeth seem ready to devour the spectator. The eyes have an evil, ambiguous expression. There are actually five eyes in the face, since the two orange spots on the nose also seem to be eyes. The motif of many eyes, a nose that appears to be an animal head, and the wide open mouth and sharp teeth appears in all three monster pictures.

Discussion

Since Matthew was not psychoanalyzed it is impossible to determine just what the monster episode had meant for him, or why it had such lasting positive effects. If we translate the symbols contained in the monster heads one by one, always remembering that any symbol may have active or passive meaning, the monster heads embody fantasies and fears of devouring and being devoured, the many eyes symbolize both the desire to see and fear of being seen. The nose which also looks like another face is probably related both to ideas of birth and ideas about the penis, especially the fantasized, hidden penis of the mother. But all this means no more than that the heads embody fantasies, theories, and fears which appear regularly in early childhood and are, like everything at this age, connected with the mother. The precise individual meaning of each symbol for Harry and later for Matthew remains obscure.

Harry and Matthew both had very disturbed mothers. Harry had painted his first monster after visiting his mother in a mental institution. Matthew's mother had kept active a symptom which belonged to Matthew's infancy. One might conjecture that in both cases the regressed and disturbed mothers kept alive primitive concepts and patterns which the children should have outgrown normally. In Harry's case it seem likely that constitutional factors favored the persistence of primitive patterns, but not enough is known for further conjectures.

Harry, at 11, seemed unevenly developed. He was advanced intellectually and possessed a sense of humor. He was able to master the mechanics of everyday life. He was overly polite, anxious to please, and afraid to show negative feelings toward persons in authority. On the other hand Harry seemed to have no concepts of the nature of other people's feelings and reactions, and there was a withdrawal into a private world where neither moral values nor the laws of nature had much meaning.

Harry painted his monsters with calm deliberation. Each head maps out his concepts and ideas with the precision of a scientific illustration. The paintings are frightening to the spectator because of the archaic and cruel ideas which they embody, but Harry did not master anxiety through painting monsters. He had established an inner balance which kept his fantasy world pleasureable and free of anxiety no matter what the content would be. His anxiety was directed outwards. Harry was overanxious to please and afraid of doing wrong, but felt no qualms about inventing the most fiendish plots or painting the most gruesome scenes. His clear and cold representations of fantasies that normally remain buried and chaotic helped other children who were haunted by vague feelings and fantasies of the same nature to give form to their ideas.

Matthew's alternating depressions and regressions during painting must have been caused by such fantasies because monsters freed him of a painting block. That it was possible for Matthew to free himself to such a great extent through just one episode of painting monsters adds weight to the conjecture that Matthew's disturbance was induced by the mother without having taken deep roots in his personality. Matthew's later painting of boats and weapons shows assertion of his manhood and independence. His subsequent development towards a greater realism and awareness of the world around him was in keeping with the emotional and developmental level of a child of his age, enhanced by more than ordinary talent and sensitivity.

The Little Boys' Monsters

It is interesting that the majority of the other children who copied Harry's monsters belonged to the youngest, most immature group. Although none of those children were below 8 years old, their developmental stage and their painting was hardly above a 4 to 6 year old level. Many of these little boys would ordinarily not permit themselves to paint according to their own level and concepts but tried to imitate the older boys. For this group Harry's example meant more freedom to paint on their own emotional level. Expression through symbols was still natural to them. Most of the monsters were supposed to be ghosts, giants, or other fearful creatures. To express cannibalistic aggressiveness by painting lots of teeth, or show fantasies of power and potency through multiplication of eyes, enormous noses, or protruding horns was in keeping with the children's developmental level. Those paintings were less monstrous as the mode of expression was a sign of immaturity, not of regression. It was, in a sense, still in the state of innocence. Harry's painting caused revulsion and uneasiness because of an uncanny combination of a mature intellect and strong talent and archaic concepts and patterns.

Edgar

Edgar's monster (Plate III colorprint) was his first completed painting. Edgar was an extremely nervous 10 year old child with exaggerated fear of the dark. He had a gift for drawing and painting but never completed anything. In spite of the bizarre, non-realistic form, the monster bears a striking resemblance to Edgar's facial expression of fast-shifting eyes and fixed toothy grin. The monster remained an isolated incident. Edgar went back to more realistic painting. His anxiety showed mainly in his people's faces. For instance, at Christmas Edgar managed to produce a Santa Claus who looked just as wide-eyed and frantic as Edgar's monster (though the painting was realistic).

Eventually Edgar gave form to his fear of the dark in a painting of a Batman (Plate IV colorprint) which so much impressed his schoolmates that it created a new fad. The painting shows a masked man, nude but for a black bathing suit, with black bat wings suspended in semi-darkness. The darkness is painted in short, rhythmic brushstrokes in many shades of green, blue, and brown, with red and orange highlights. The colors recall a tempestuous night as it is revealed by flashes of lightning. The painting is filled with anxiety. The Batman seems the least frightening part of the painting. It is Edgar himself suspended in darkness surrounded by nameless fears. The Batman is on a much higher emotional level than the monster.

At the time of the monster Harry's example had freed Edgar to project his personality in a kind of self-portrait expressed in the primitive symbolic language which alone was at his disposal. As Edgar was moving on towards a higher integration the monster remained a single incident and Edgar went back to struggling with more realistic painting. Eventually he reached a point where again he could express very personal matter, but this time without need for private symbolism. Instead a mood was created by subtle shades of color applied with deliberate concentration. The Batman, though winged and masked, is essentially human. There is a fuller identification between painter and his painting. Although fears and disturbances persist, they are more internalized and more accessible to treatment. Edgar took the form for his Batman from the vulgar and cruel images of comic books, but transformed them and gave them new meaning.

Through Edgar's painting the figure of Batman became popular among those children who had a need to express the dark, sinister side of life. Edgar's painting differed greatly in quality from Harry's monsters. His influence reached a slightly different section of the population and gave their production a different starting point. Thus in some of the children's versions the Batman lost the integration which Edgar's painting had reached and became more monstrous and more filled with symbolism.

In spite of their differences Harry's and Edgar's painting had enough in common to act as catalysts for emotions and problems of the same general order. We see a circle completed, and a new circle beginning in the steady change of patterns and forms which keeps the production of a community alive and moving.

Harry's Later Development

Harry's influence did not last very long. When monster painting went out of fashion the community reacted with a vague sense of guilt and uneasiness about the episode. Harry's painting was now criticized with remarks like, "All you can do is paint monsters." The criticism came at a good time. Harry was getting ready to question his own behavior and ideas. He was beginning to explore what it felt like to be a boy among boys. He gradually lost interest in painting. His loss of interest in art seemed a healthy sign. It probably did not mean that his fantasies had ceased or had changed character, but it meant that the reality of his life at the school, with its many activities and excitements, was taking precedence over daydreaming. Harry's fantasies found a more constructive outlet in newspaper work. He became editor of the school's paper and wrote stories and editorials. He developed a weird sense of humor which made his bizarre stories more acceptable. If we want to be optimistic we may picture Harry growing up into a man with a sense of humor in the tradition of those humorists such as Charles Adams or James Thurber, who play upon the juxtaposition of the laws of reason and reality and the workings of the unconscious mind. In those creations the bizarre and cruel fantasies of childhood are made acceptable by their very absurdity in the light of reason, while, in turn, the inexorable laws of reason and reality seem ponderous and ridiculous as they are played against the deeper verity of the unconscious mind. But these conjectures lead too far afield from the present topic of investigation.

Discussion

The passage on monsters has been longer and more involved than the stories of Kings and Prisoners. In those two examples emotionally loaded subject matter was followed up as it emerged through the initiative of gifted children and was transformed and varied by others. The passage on monsters has for its subject the world of the irrational and its language of symbols and images as it takes form in bizarre and imaginative painting.

If we compare the pictures of Kings and Prisoners, or for that matter, any of the other reproductions in this book, with the section on monsters (Figs. 2, 3, 4, 5, 6, 13, 14 and Plate III), we feel as if we had entered another world. Even the haunting despair and violence of Walter's prisoner is expressed in an emotional language which differs essentially from the horror and anxiety of Clyde's black face or Edgar's frantic monster. The two kinds of painting are separated by the same gulf which divides primitive art, even of the highest artistic merit, from art that is no longer primitive. This statement has value only as an analogy because children's art should never be equated with the art of adults even if the adults are primitives

Our children's monster painting is stark, at times moving, often highly decorative, and not quite human. While the first impression is strong, often shocking, the paintings do not stand up well against time. Their message is simple, they seem to lack depth, and, as shock wears off, they lose much of their interest and meaning.

All paintings described contain stark, unbridled aggression. Their language of expression consists largely of symbols. For instance, in all the monster faces each organ has symbolic meaning while its realistic functioning is disregarded. Thus the double row of teeth in Clyde's face (Fig. 2) suffices to symbolize devouring aggression. Anatomical verity such as addition of lips or jaws would be superfluous. The fear of being watched and fantasies of having power to see and penetrate all secrets can be expressed by multiplying the number of eyes, as in Harry's and Matthew's monsters (Figs. 13 and 14), since eyes are not conceived as organs of the human body but as symbols only.

The completed paintings consist largely of arrangements of parts which retain their symbolic autonomy. They consist, so to speak, of one layer only. If we probe below their symbolic meaning, we immediately reach the primary process, the raw impulses and urges charged with unbridled aggression beyond the ego's control and influence. The paintings appear to be not quite human because the ego is only in the process of being formed. The pattern of symbols appears to be the first thin layer of structurization which is formed to bind and control the primeval forces. Thus we find the symbol at the beginning of all cultural endeavor, and again invariably at the bottom of all cultural and artistic achievement.

Because the monster paintings have one emotional layer only, their form remains flat. Space, volume, and transitions which lead the spectator beyond the two-dimensional surface are absent since that which occurs beyond this surface remains chaotic and uncommunicable. Their flatness gives the paintings a resemblance to purely decorative art which also is two-dimensional, though for different reasons. Decorative painting remains flat because its function is limited to adding interest and value to objects of practical use. The decorative artist who leads the spectator beyond the immediately visible detracts from his object and defeats his purpose. Decorative art remains flat because emotional depth has no place in decoration. The monster paintings are also two-dimensional but charged with powerful emotions. In this context it is interesting to note that the only decoration which can be considered genuine art as compared to applied art occurs in primitive cultures, especially in primitive pottery. As long as emotionally charged content is expressed in two-dimensional symbolic language the artist can paint his message on a pot without breaking the continuity of the surface of his vessel.

Returning to our children, we find that we have acquired a better understanding of the emotional basis of certain common formal elements. But there are other qualities in the paintings which differ substantially from child to child. Above all there is a difference in regard to anxiety. For instance Harry's and Matthew's monsters are frightening but do not express the painter's anxiety. Paul's creatures also seem free of anxiety. Clyde's and Edgar's work, on the other hand, expresses tremendous anxiety.

If we compare the children's personalities as far as this can be done without deep analysis, Clyde and Edgar appear to be overwhelmed by their impulses and fantasies and to be experiencing guilt and anxiety on behalf of them. Their fear of the dark is fear of their masturbatory fantasies and of their dreams which make them appear in their own eyes as evil, demonic beings who, by the law of Talion, will be punished by the same horrors which they evoke in their sadistic and masochistic fantasies. Their paintings express at once the pleasures which the fantasies contain, the child's guilt, and the attempt at mastering the conflict. Since the child has reached a stage of development where his archaic concepts and pleasures appear incongrous and monstrous to the ego, treatment should bring about a gradual disappearance of the fantasies and anxiety, and with it a change of style in art. Actually this development occurred. Both Clyde's and Edgar's painting changed towards a more highly structured, more "human" style.

Harry's and Paul's paintings are very different again. Those two children had established an inner balance which kept their fantasy world free of guilt. Anxiety is, of course, not entirely absent. For instance, Harry's monsters or his instruments of murder contain fear of being devoured or being killed. But the concepts themselves do not seem monstrous to the child's ego. The ego seems to accept ideas of devouring and being devoured, of killing and torture and aggression. In other words, the ego accepts the primary process, as long as it all remains fantasy. Aggressive acts, even on a small scale, evoke great anxiety, both because of Harry's underlying savage aggression and because of his primitive concepts of retaliation and punishment which would make all acts of aggression very dangerous indeed in Harry's world.

Paul had less fear of his own aggressive acts, but then his fantasy world was also less savage. Still it is characteristic of Paul's kind of personality that he could not tolerate aggression and hostility in persons in authority. Paul was extremely sensitive to the timbre of people's voices. Even to slight irritation and hostility in a voice he reacted with a wooden expression and complete withdrawal. Actual screaming could bring about one of his rare attacks of irrational, destructive fury.

In Harry or Paul's case no basic change could be expected unless a complete change of character structure occurred. With increasing maturity and development of those faculties that are directed towards reality and relationships certain changes might take place.

In Harry's case we could foresee a lessening of interest in the fantasies so that the whole world of the irrational seems less real, even at times absurd to the healthy part of the child's personality. Thus we could picture Harry developing a sense of humor which would contain his bizarre fantasies, even rendering them pleasurable. But although there are indications of such a development, the outlook remains uncertain and the picture we are painting an optimistic conjecture.

The development which might be anticipated in Paul's painting seems much harder to put into words. Paul's great gift as a painter defies analysis and explanation. As this great talent, this capacity for sublimation, acts upon material which remains primitive and subject to the primary process, a transformation takes place which is hard to define. It recalls qualities in the work of Paul Klee or in Lewis Carrol's *Alice in Wonderland*. (There is, of course, no intention of putting Paul's work on a level with those great artists.) The paintings do not acquire three-dimensional substance, but a kind of transparency which adds a new dimension so that our characterization of a flat, two-dimensional style no longer quite holds true. The world which is created remains bizarre, aggression is rampant, reason and reality meaningless. Still there is sublimation. The painter's world no longer shocks and frightens. The paintings do not awaken tendencies toward uncontrolled regression. The fantastic world has become accessible and pleasure can be gained from the experience.

Again we have overshot the mark and created an optimistic picture foreseeing a development which is still in its infancy. It remains dubious whether a delinquent child, of limited intelligence, committed to a life of poverty and cultural deprivation could fulfill the promise of a great talent which seems incongrous in relation to his other mental capacities.

The closer analysis of the group of monster paintings shows an absence of rigid boundaries. Mutual influences, borrowing of subject matter and styles cut across personality differences. The art therapist's attitude towards the painting therefore remains flexible. As therapist she has above all to help every child to realize his painting, regardless of subject matter or style. She has to help the anxiety-ridden child to give form to his anxiety, or help the cold, cruel painter to get his ideas on paper.

On the other hand it has to be borne in mind that much of the children's disturbance is due to the primitive and seductive personalities of their parents. (Matthew's mother is an extreme example of this kind of seduction.) It is therefore very important that the therapist should not appear to the child as another seductive adult who will push him deeper into regression. The therapist's understanding and acceptance of his work should never appear to the child as a ghoulish kind of pleasure in the cruelty and aggression which is brought to light. The best guide to handling those extremely subtle problems lies in observation of the children's moods during the session.

For instance when Matthew painted his monsters he was in an elated and productive mood. Matthew's monsters were much more primitive than his general level of development. Still Matthew was not just regressing as he painted them, rather he was bringing to light something which had existed within him much like a foreign body and had to come to the surface before it could be rejected.

A child who is regressing and painting monsters to show his aggression and disgust would be in a different mood. He would be irritable and hostile and, as the mood gathered momentum, his aggression would rarely remain confined to his painting. At such a time the art therapist steps in and leads the child back to more constructive work, or discontinues the child's session.

The question could be posed whether the therapist should not at times attempt to create certain situations. For instance, as painting monsters was so helpful to Matthew, should not the therapist have brought about a situation instead of depending on a happy coincidence?

The main obstacle would be that, unless the child were being analyzed and the art therapist working closely with the analyst, there would be no way of determining the right moment and method for such a step. Relying on intuition can be treacherous. There would be any amount of danger of stepping in at the wrong moment and appearing to the child as the brutal, seductive adult whom he fears and distrusts.

In general it seems best to use intuition only in the handling of situations as they arise and to trust the children's instinct for finding ways of using any number of different situations for communication.

REALITY, RELATIONSHIPS, AND SUBJECT MATTER

Of all the paintings that have been described and reproduced so far, only two pictures show a child's immediate environment, Plate I and Figure 8, by Martin. Plate I is a portrait of Martin's mother; Figure 8, a drawing of his home street, with himself represented as a tiny figure flying a kite on his roof. The portrait was painted 6 months before his discharge, when Martin's relationship to the mother had undergone important changes. Martin, who previously had not been able to conceive of himself as an individual separate from his mother, had found his independence and had even rejected certain ideas and attitudes that she had implanted in him. Consequently he was now able to understand and accept his mother as an individual and to represent her in a painting. The drawing of the city street was done on the train which took him home to live with his parents. He represents the crowded confining street but still asserts his strength and individuality by flying a kite high into the free sky. The environment to which Martin was returning seemed far from ideal, but Martin's painting indicated that as far as his own inner health was concerned he was ready to live in a family situation. No child newly arrived at the school could have produced those two pictures.

As a rule the children's former lives, their families and homes, the streets they used to play on, their schools, teachers, toys, and pets never appear in painting. The symbolic expression of fantasies and theories concerning the mystery of birth and sex are rare. Family relationships are seldom expressed, and female figures rarely appear in painting. Of the new experiences which the school offers, only a narrow selection is reflected in occasional paintings. The school's horses are painted most frequently. There are also some paintings of the buildings and of the truck and bus, and of cars owned by staff members. Exciting and pleasant activities such as swimming, fishing, horseback riding, sports, and games also occasionally find their way into pictures.

Experiences are more often expressed by projection into a more glamorous setting. For instance a field day at the school may bring a harvest of paintings of champion sportsmen but rarely a single picture of boys running or playing games. The children's affection for the horses may inspire romantic pictures of cowboy life and of wild horses, but seldom paintings of boys riding or taking care of horses.

But even such projections and glamorized elaborations of experience are comparatively rare. A great deal of all painting is totally divorced from everyday life. Much of it is based on the ready-made daydreams of comic books, movies, and television. Also there are many paintings just of symbols such as hearts, crosses, shields, swords, knives, etc.

Although a preference for symbols and for romantic elaborations would be part of the children's developmental stage, the almost total avoidance of everyday life, the avoidance of self-representation except in disguise, and, above all, the lack of representation of relationships (except for fights between two adversaries there are very few paintings wherein more than one person is represented) has to be understood as an indication of the children's isolation and disturbance.

PLATE I. Size, 12 x 18 inches, tempera (detail).

PLATE II. Size, 24 x 36 inches, tempera.

PLATE III. Size, 12 x 18 inches, tempera.

PLATE IV. Size, 12 x 18 inches, tempera.

PLATE V. Size, 18 x 24 inches, tempera.

PLATE VI. Size, 24 x 30 inches, tempera.

PLATE VII. Size, 24 x 36 inches, tempera.

PLATE VIII. Size, 24 x 30 inches, tempera.

The paintings which have been described and analyzed demonstrate very graphically the children's confusion, the barrenness of their lives, and the insoluble conflicts which surround them. We have seen how all mankind, including their own selves, appears to some of them as a monstrous conglomeration of unrelated parts filled with primitive urges. The prisoners have shown the overwhelming difficulties which confront the boys as they contemplate their position in society and their future lives, and the kings shows the rigidity and remoteness of the ego ideals of those children who are striving towards concepts of human dignity and self-esteem.

If the children turn towards a world of primitive symbols and daydreams, this cannot be understood simply as an escape from an unpleasant reality, although there is, of course, also escape. In many cases the children's personalities are so unformed that they lack the feeling of self-identity and completeness which should be necessary for absorbing experiences and giving them back in a coherent form. Those children are haunted by a feeling of emptiness and isolation. Behind some of the stereotyped swords and shields, skulls and crossbones, hearts, crosses, octopuses or Indian chiefs, there hides not just a frightened little boy who is disguising himself as a big, powerful man, but a bundle of confusion and contradiction which has not yet formed into an individual. Drawing a human figure, however primitive, would be an impossible and frightening task for a child whose body image is still unformed and incomplete. A child's clinging to simple symbolic shapes such as a cross or a shield or heart is often a first attempt at creating something of his own which symbolizes and proves his existence.

A child might take up painting shields and cling to the subject for weeks or months. As he perfects his shields, and his schoolmates admire them the child begins to think of himself as the famous painter of shields. The shield then serves to define his personality and give him a feeling of individual existence. This process becomes even more effective when a group of children begin to elaborate on a theme.

At one time a group of very immature children took up painting the symbols of the playing cards with great enthusiasm. Their red and black spades, diamonds, hearts, and clubs were soon enlivened by any variety of color; arrangements and designs appeared which bore little resemblance to any conventional card. As painting proceeded each version increasingly expressed the painter's personality. Eventually the more creative children ventured beyond the symbols and began using the kings and queens of cards as subjects. Some children followed suit; others stuck to their hearts and spades, and so the transition to more creative painting was made by those who were ready for it.

Through experiences of this kind the children's feeling of identity begins to crystallize. As the group freely elaborates on the same subject, both the experience of resemblances and the discovery of individual differences in their paintings serve to define their individuality. It would be hard to determine just how much of this process could be called identification, and how much remains at the preliminary state of imitation. In either case the experience contributes to the process of identification and to the development of a feeling of identity.

As the childrens' personalities crystallize, conventional stereotypes and rigid symbols recede. With the emergence of a body image people and animals can be represented and subject matter becomes richer and more lively. But the children's isolation, bitterness and disappointment with their families, and a feeling of worthlessness persist. To be a child means to be exposed to abandonment, brutality, and seduction. Self-representation or representation of family life remains impossible. Paintings are filled with dreams of power and revenge, and hate and fear are the prevailing emotions.

Sharks, eagles, octopuses, wild animals, gangsters, strongmen, and other dangerous and ferocious figures abound in their painting. A preference for the underwater world or for rocketships and Marsmen expresses the children's estrangement from reality. Often a desire for security, peace, and love can be expressed only in impersonal conventional forms such as paintings of horses, trees, and flowers or landscapes.

Those children who are finding their way back to reality and relationship often begin by representing the positive experiences at the school. A new feeling of mastery and pleasure in his own person may come to a child as he learns to swim and dive, becomes an expert horseback rider, fisherman, or painter. When a group of boys were preparing for a diving and swimming performance for which they trained regularly at a Y.M.C.A. swimming pool, many of them began painting divers and swimmers in various positions. Their own kinesthetic sense helped them in representing the actions of their divers. All the Negro boys painted their figures brown without hesitation. The boys' satisfaction with the mastery of their own bodies made romantic trappings unnecessary. None of the divers was jumping into the water in order to battle with sharks and octopuses. Background scenes were pleasant and peaceful.

Country life and a closer acquaintance with animals often helps children to express new positive feelings through pictures of animal life, such as birds hatching eggs or feeding their young, or scenes of horses and deer. The role of the male as protector and the tender relationship between the mare and her colt can be painted at a time when it would still be impossible for the child to express the same feelings in human shape. Indeed a child who was able to paint such a scene undisguised should not remain in an institutional setting, and this stage of development leads beyond the limitations of this study.

Summarizing, we can say that the children's isolation and their lack of feeling of identity vary in degree, but that there is no boy at the school who could fully accept himself as a child or accept his family, in particular, his mother. The children's fantasy life remains isolated from their everyday experiences, and fusion between reality and fantasy is only occasionally reached. Consequently, if we compare the boys' production with paintings of less disturbed children with the same opportunity for creative work, we find just as much talent and at times a greater intensity in our children's paintings, but a comparative narrowness and barrenness in subject matter. Additional reasons for those limitations are the cultural poverty of the children's environments, and the artificial conditions of a boys' school where the boys' ideas and preoccupations tend to become narrower and more compulsive without challenge and inspiration from the other sex.

The fusion of reality and fantasy depends both on the positive experiences which life at the school offers, and on the child's capacity for absorbing them. A good example of the mechanisms and conflicts involved is the children's painting of horses.

By giving the children horses to ride, feed, and groom, the school offers the children an entirely new, pleasant experience. Their relationship to the horses is not burdened with the painful and bitter associations that overshadow all relationships to human beings. For many children the relationship to the horses remains singularly free of ambivalence and guilt. Often they provide a unique medium for experimenting with a precarious capacity for relationship.

The school's horses seldom appear directly in painting. Even the children who are ready to draw from nature and who go out to sketch the horses readily translate their sketches into romantic paintings of groups of wild horses or cowboys' horses or even unicorns. Such romantic elaborations do not constitute a denial of reality. Rather there is a fusion of reality and fantasy akin to the painting of less disturbed children. Gestures and attitudes that have been observed among the horses are easily incorporated in pictures. Horses are often painted in pairs, leaning their heads together in a friendly fashion. They are painted grazing and feeding alone or in families. Portraits of beautiful horses' heads express an admiration mixed with tenderness which is rarely expressed in paintings of human beings.

In general, even though the horse constitutes a symbol of power and potency, it remains free of the sadistic aggressive component of more primitive phallic symbols. This, of course, does not hold true of every horse that is painted at the school. In the hands of the more primitive and hostile children a horse may attain the ferocity of a dragon.

A child's increasing acceptance of reality and the formation of positive relationships may be expressed in art through any number of subjects.

Carl, Figure 9, began by painting kings. Those paintings were followed by paintings of Negro sportsmen and Negro dancers, and eventually Carl was able to paint a picture of teen-agers like himself dancing at a party. Matthew, Figures 14 and 15, was only moderately interested in horses but became very absorbed in sketching trees, flowers, and buildings. In practical life Matthew became interested in growing things, and gardening became a bond between him and a number of boys who shared his interest. For Fletcher carpentry was his most important link to reality and relationships. He worshipped his shop teacher and maintained friendships with a number of maintenance men. Before his discharge Fletcher painted a book of tools with the name of each tool printed below. For a group of swimmers mastery over their bodies led to self-representation in art.

In each case a development towards self-acceptance and capacity for relationship brings about a greater awareness of reality and with it a change of subject matter and style. Such a development need not necessarily lead to a naturalistic style in painting. The formal language of a child's work depends on his age and developmental stage, and an 8 year old will express reality and relationships differently from a 12 or 13 year old.

The development is possible only when continuous positive reality experiences are available. Ultimately no amount of symbolic activities such as painting, music, or imaginative play can be truly meaningful to the child unless they are nourished by tangible constructive experiences in practical life.

THE LEARNING PROCESS

Art therapy is not a subject to be taught formally in the sense in which reading and writing or crafts can be taught. It also is not identical with the teaching of art where the children's progress as painters is the main concern. Yet art therapy includes a continuous learning process. Most of the children are not much aware of their inner lives and have not learned to express their feelings in any but the most primitive, undifferentiated ways. Through their painting the children learn to know themselves better. They become acquainted with their likes and dislikes, and, as they develop an individual style of painting, they learn to understand and accept themselves.

The creative process is inseparable from the painter's craft. As they express themselves through paint, the children acquire skill in handling their medium, they learn to control their impulses and tempers. They have to learn to concentrate on their task and to be patient with themselves and others. In this learning process the art therapist becomes the teacher and educator.

Learning does not come easily to children who have had very few constructive learning experiences since their earliest childhood. Most of the children have failed at school, and there have been far too few occasions for informal learning by taking part in productive work such as children in rural communities experience.

Learning is the greatest experience of childhood. Deprivation of means for sublimation and channeling of energies into constructive work is at least as harmful for the growing child as deprivation of material and instinctual needs. The child who cannot use the learning situation in the classroom and is still forced to spend long hours in idleness and boredom is subject to the frustration and helpless rage which deprivation of any strong urge brings about. A child's disruptive behavior is then not only the result of his immaturity and impulsiveness, but equally a result of his thwarted need for constructive learning experiences. And so memories of frustration and rage caused by enforced idleness combine with memories of failure, embarrassment and punishment to make the whole area of book learning distasteful to the child.

A child who is unable to learn in the classroom needs other learning experiences. As long as learning continues in other areas, a child's development need not be seriously stunted. Children who are unwilling to learn to read may still become capable carpenters and craftsmen, they may learn on the farm, develop as painters, musicians, and so forth. Success in those fields may eventually lessen a resistance against academics.

Unfortunately there are in our culture no experiences that can quite substitute for reading. Reading is so indispensable for orientation and for mastery of most other skills that illiteracy amounts almost to a physical handicap which hampers and stunts the child's growth at every turn. No matter how defiantly he may act, the feeling of failure and incompleteness of the illiterate child once he has past the lower grades often overshadows the attitude towards all learning, especially when conceptual thought is required.

In the children's minds art is not associated with school. Conflicts and preoccupations with fantasies are less of a handicap in art, where they can be expressed, than in academic subjects which require concentration that excludes fantasizing and day dreaming. The children are starved for constructive and creative experiences and generally eager to come to art sessions. Still the children bring to the learning situation in art all the resistances, defenses, and evasive tactics which they have developed against all learning.

Many children are eager to come to art, but once confronted with the actual task of painting a picture, their chief concern is not to commit themselves. Expecting failure from the beginning, they will use any tactics to prevent the therapist and themselves from ascertaining just what they can or can't do, creating a deadlock for progress.

Seeing that the teacher can paint well, some children will distort the learning process into a dogged attempt at appropriating her skill, much as if it were a material possession which the therapist refuses to part with. A child then will not just attempt to make the therapist help him, but will try to make her act in his stead, and carry out his intentions as if she were his alter ego, capable of reading his mind, or even capable of giving form to his vague and incomplete ideas. In the attempt to accomplish this feat a child may try all available methods: violence, cunning, flattery, or whatever may seem to work. There is only one thing he would not do, and that is to attempt to draw or paint himself. Sometimes the pattern may be more passive and a child may become completely dependent, expecting to acquire skill and knowledge as if by magic. Upon the discovery that the therapist cannot help him in this way, he may react with outraged indignation, as to a personal injury.

In either case the art of painting is conceived almost as a material substance, which the therapist is able to give or to withhold according to her wishes. Except for the element of cunning and worldly shrewdness typical of the delinquent, the attitude is close to the concepts of the very young child who still feels one with the mother and is unable to distinguish between the self and the outside world. At this period everything good or bad seems to come from her, every frustration caused by her withholding of fulfillment, and every pleasure the result of her love and bounty.

Vestiges of this magic interpretation of the teachers' powers and function would be part of any relationship between student and teacher. Although the art therapist has neither the power of magically influencing the child's painting skill or his mood, nor the ability to read the child's mind, her experience enables her to anticipate many difficulties, and she will frequently guess a child's intentions and ideas fairly accurately. Knowing a child well, a teacher can find ways of adapting her teaching to the child's personality and understanding.

When children feel understood by the teacher and respond with some measure of confidence and trust, their reactions will be a mixture of patterns belonging to different developmental stages and very infantile responses will coexist with more mature ones. So much remains unconscious and indefinable in the transmission of skills, knowledge, and attitudes which we call teaching, that a feeling of the magical or miraculous is part of all learning that goes beyond the mechanical storing up of facts. The mastery of skills or discovery of truth affords a sense of elation and increased power that may seem short of miraculous, and so, in the last analysis, every teacher remains something of a witch or wizard to the student. Thus, underlying the more mature identification with the teacher and the rational assimilation of her subject, there remains the primitive idea of taking possession of the teacher's person and of her magic powers. In the process

The Learning Process

of learning and growing up, the more primitive concepts gradually recede. Among disturbed and immature children this process will be slower and more difficult.

In general we can say that the children bring to the learning situation their innate need for growth, the inquisitiveness and delight in new discoveries, and the desire for mastery of the environment which belongs to childhood. At the same time they approach learning with a sense of failure and deep distrust in their own abilities. This fills them with hate and distrust of people who seem to be bent on leading them into disastrous experiences of failure and defeat. In this sense the art therapist appears as a dangerous person who is forcing them to face a discrepancy between their dreams of grandeur and a reality that will reduce them to nothingness. Finally, they bring to learning their impulsiveness and immaturity, and with it concepts and mechanisms belonging to a stage where identification and self-identification are not fully achieved. In addition, each child is burdened with his personal history of frustrations, disappointments, and traumatic experiences which make him a difficult partner in any life situation.

In spite of all hindrances, the desire to produce persists, and with it the possibility for success and growth. In this process the art therapist will mean to the children many things. She may be the envied possessor of magical skills, the voice of conscience and reason, the guide towards pleasure and success, or the hated intruder who is bent on embarrassing and defeating the child, and so forth. This transference situation should remain centered around the child's production. This means that the relationship remains less intimate than the relationship to the psychotherapist or social worker. If the child acts out too much of his early conflicts with the art therapist, his production suffers and still the acting out does not help to solve the child's troubles. The deepest level of communication between child and therapist should be reached through the child's painting and the therapist's sharing and understanding of the productive process. In the child's eyes the art therapist remains a special kind of teacher, whose subject defies teaching by set rules and rigid standards of accomplishment. Still it should be clear that art sessions are not times of free play, but periods devoted to creative work that requires effort and concentration and should lead to progress and growth.

SUCCESS AND GROWTH

The great hindrance to learning is the children's low tolerance for any kind of failure or frustration. The slightest mistake will easily convince a child that his effort is wholly worthless. One of the art therapist's main occupations consists of rescuing pictures that would be destroyed for minor reasons. Again and again it has to be demonstrated to the children that mistakes are not irreparable and that the therapist is willing and able to help at all times. To keep the child from regression, some measure of success has to be assured at any cost. Pleasure and success remain the great incentives for growth. When neglect and lack of constructive experiences are the main cause of a child's immaturity, growth can often be very rapid, especially when the child is still young.

Jacky

Jacky and his fraternal twin Richard came to the school at the age of 9. They were neglected children who had received little care or training of any kind. Jacky was the smaller and younger-looking of the twins. In art Jacky was at a total loss. His few independent attempts at drawing produced the kind of oval and circular shapes characteristic of a child's earliest scribblings. In his helplessness Jacky expected the teacher to draw and paint for him. His behavior was alternately demanding and defiant and frustrations enraged him.

The first change occurred before Thanksgiving and centered around food. Jacky came to the art session with the intention of painting a big turkey on a platter, to be hung up in his group's living room. Jacky could be persuaded to draw the platter. Here he could use the oval shapes which came natural to him. The therapist had to draw the turkey, but Jacky was ready to draw potatoes and radishes, and here again he could use his round shapes. Fired by success and the thought of good food, he also added carrots and celery, a glass of milk and rolls. He colored the picture with great enthusiasm and without smearing and developed more skill than he had seemed capable of previously. Jacky painted several replicas of the turkey. Each time the therapist had to help with the bird, but Jacky did the rest, depending only on praise and encouragement from the therapist.

The experience was the beginning of a rapid development in which Jacky's behavior changed as radically as his attitude toward learning. In the turkey painting the therapist had not substituted for Jacky, but for the first time Jacky and the therapist had cooperated on a common task. (The fact that the picture had been about food was probably also significant for an underfed, deprived child.) Soon Jacky ventured beyond turkeys and foods, and painted castles, boats, stars, and other things. He soon acquired the form perception and muscular control necessary for his new subjects. With success Jacky's behavior changed. He was less demanding, became cooperative and able to wait his turn. His rages and verbal abuses diminished. The same kind of transformation took place in the classroom. When his understanding and patient teacher found ways to help Jacky to some initial success, he changed from a savage little demon into an eager child who delighted in his new powers.

In this context it is interesting to note that Jacky was just as much enraged by the wrong kind of help as by no help at all. On several occasions a young student tried to help Jacky with his pictures. Her drawing was too small and complex for Jacky's understanding. He was bewildered and needed her constant help. This enraged him to a point where he abused and tortured the student throughout the art session.

Although Jacky received insufficient care and training at home, he had been given some measure of love and affection from the mother, who had preferred him to his twin brother. Jacky's need for learning and growth had been frustrated, but his self-confidence and capacity for relationships were not seriously damaged. Therefore Jacky could recapture the missing experiences with relatively little difficulty.

Richard

Jacky's twin brother Richard was more seriously damaged. Richard was taller, handsomer, and neater in appearance than Jacky, but Jacky seems to have been from the beginning the warmer, more outgoing child. The mother's preference for Jacky may have been a response to an initial difference, and her coldness to Richard may in turn have increased his withdrawal and passivity. But all this remains conjecture.

Richard's first paintings were more skillful than Jacky's earliest attempts. They also indicated more disturbance. Richard's first picture consisted of two heads, one white and one brown. Later he covered one sheet with four heads, two of them white-skinned, two brown. The same division appeared in other contexts, for instance, in a painting of a shark divided vertically so that head and front were grey and the hind part white. A slight difference in the twins' skin color (Jacky's was a little lighter than Richard's) may have added to Richard's tendency to divide the world into dark and light, but could not have caused the division.

In general Richard did not paint much. What little time he spent in the art room was devoted to salvaging other children's discarded pictures, which he completed or simply hoarded. Richard was evasive and passive and could not be motivated to do much work. He needed success just as badly as Jacky, but, while Jacky's hostility and lack of confidence had disappeared with the first rays of success, Richard's feeling of worthlessness, his distrust and hostility, were more deep-seated. Richard could not be pleased with anything he did. Positive experiences had to be introduced slowly, by overlooking hostility and behavior problems, and by partly giving in to his parasitic collecting of pictures. When Richard eventually was ready to disclose more of his own ideas, his painting showed much anxiety and distortion. It seemed evident that Richard's treatment would require the joint efforts of the staff for a long time to come.

Since at the present time Richard's treatment has not progressed beyond the earliest stages, the story remains inconclusive. It was chosen to demonstrate the difference between deprivation of constructive experiences and deprivation of love. Richard's story illustrates how difficult it is to give children whose most basic needs have been frustrated any incentive for progress or any pleasure in success.

PERCEPTION AND SKILL

When Jacky, who had never painted in his life, began to paint, his first attempts were on a 2 to 3 year old level. His visual images were vague as he had never tried to put them on paper, yet Jacky did not see the world as it would appear to a 2 or 3 year old child. Jacky's painting was below his general state of development. Within a few months Jacky's painting matured to a 6 to 7 year old level, and this reflected his actual retardation (he was then $9\frac{1}{2}$ years old). When a child's painting fails to do justice to his ideas, because of too great a discrepancy between the child's perception and his technical skill and painting experience, this can be so maddening that it may discourage all further attempts. In such a situation the therapist will help the boy as much as possible to catch up with himself and to acquire the missing technique and experience. If necessary, she will substitute for the child, help him with his paintings so that he may have the satisfaction of seeing his ideas take form even at a time when his lack of practice would make it impossible for him to succeed alone.

Walter

Walter, who is known to the reader as the painter of a prisoner (Plate II colorprint), came to the school at the age of $9\frac{1}{2}$. From the beginning Walter was attracted to art and desperately wanted to paint well. He had a fertile imagination and clear visual images, but lacked practice and technical skill. It was hard for Walter to submit to the discipline of learning. Failure enraged him, and his first weeks and months in the art room were marked by frequent explosions and tantrums. Still Walter did not resist the learning process itself. He did not hide his failures or try to appropriate other people's work. Walter's ambitions were focused on realizing his visions. Even when he was not able to produce the effects he wanted, he could communicate his ideas to the therapist, and when she helped him she accepted only those contributions which fulfilled his ideas. As soon as Walter had grasped a concept, he was eager to take over. Soon he acquired the technical skill he needed to give form to a wealth of ideas. Walter's emotionality made working with him difficult at all times. Still Walter's learning ability had remained unimpaired by his disturbances and teaching could be straightforward and to the point.

Ralph

Not all children have Walter's initiative and creative urge. Ralph was not unwilling to learn, nor were his ambitions too far ahead of his abilities, but Ralph had spent many years in hospitals and lacked initiative and daring. He painted mostly small seascapes and loved combinations of different shades of blue with white. Ralph could not work by himself. At each step he needed the stimulation and reassurance of the therapist's participation. He had clear visual images of the pictures he wanted to paint and could explain to the therapist just what he wanted her to do, but he would take over by himself only when he was certain of success. Ralph was a patient worker who had much taste and a great love for pictures. In the course of time he managed to learn to work more independently. His painting never attained much variety or emotional depth. His limitations as a painter reflected a personality that was not seriously disturbed but seemed impoverished and limited by years of empty institutional existence.

PRETENSE AND SELF-ACCEPTANCE

Jacky, Walter, and Ralph were struggling to reach their own individual levels. It was possible therefore to help them by giving assistance in technical difficulties and by substituting for them when they could not quite succeed by themselves.

Often children's ambitions are totally unrelated to their developmental stage or their own perceptions. A very immature child may want to paint like an adult or like the most advanced painter at the school and refuse to accept anything else for himself. Such children copy pictures mechanically or beg the more advanced painters to draw for them and will laboriously color those drawings without the faintest understanding of their formal language.

A little story will illustrate the point. Frank had traced a picture of a cowboy lassoing a horse, which he had found in a book. The tracing was full of complex foreshortenings beyond Frank's understanding, and he was having a hard time figuring out what colors to paint which areas. Ronny, 9 years old, saw Frank's picture, admired it, and began to "copy" it. His version showed a little man with a big cowboy hat, and a thick rope ending in a loop extending from his outstretched arm. Beside him stood a little horse in profile. Ronny had painted what he had perceived—a man lassoing a horse—and had put it in the formal language of a 9 year old child.

When a child's ambitions bear no relation to his actual self, the art therapist will do her best to help him find a starting point closer to his developmental stage. Usually it would be both impossible and unwise to force a child to face the full impact of the discrepancy between his pretenses and his actual self, and compromises must be found.

For instance, it may be possible to persuade a boy who has salvaged a picture and is finishing it to add some details of his own, such as houses, trees, or clouds. A child whose confused body image makes it impossible for him to draw or paint people, may be persuaded to concentrate on subjects like shields and swords, etc., which do not require the same degree of orientation. Occasionally a child may be willing to alternate between copying and painting his own pictures.

Such compromise experiences may prove to the child that he is more capable than he expected, so that he may venture to work more independently. Or a child's skill might improve to a point where the initial discrepancy between his ambitions and his capacities would be less striking. Ultimately a change would depend on a change in the child's self-esteem and self-acceptance, and with it on his general improvement.

The first steps toward self-reliance are memorable to every child. To give the event its full importance the therapist will tell and retell the story of his change and growth to the child whenever an opportunity arises. Once a child feels secure in his new independence, he often marks the event by discarding all pictures which he copied or salvaged or with which he received too much help from the therapist. Such a gesture does not imply that the child would from then on no longer depend on the teacher, cease all pretending, and become self-reliant. But his point of departure from now on would be his own self and his own perceptions, rather than borrowed standards and ideas.

Progress then becomes possible. The new situation brings new problems and difficulties for the painter.

Once a child's paintings are truly his own, they reflect not only his wishes and fantasies, but also his innermost feelings about himself. Any painting is in a sense a self-portrait. A child who is weak and anxious will find his weakness and fear reflected in his people. He may adorn his hero with knives, swords, big hats and buttons of any number, color, and size, thus giving him symbols of power and potency, but his hero's hands and feet will almost inevitably be tiny and weak, reflecting the child's actual helplessness. An Indian chief's face may be adorned with ferocious war paint, or a pirate may wear an exquisite moustache. Still the man's eyes, nose, and mouth will be small and weak. Such revelations of one's own weakness are frightening. Often even rather independent children will borrow the therapist's strength to give their heroes more substance or greater masculinity. Hands and feet require assistance most frequently. Often there are requests for the therapist to make a man's features older and stronger-looking, since so few of the boys can accept the fact that they are still children. As the children's inner security increases, their need for external attributes of power diminishes, and with it their need for borrowed images and borrowed strength.

CONTINUITY AND GROWTH

We have mentioned before that the children's paintings are collected in individual folders. During art sessions the children are free to look at their folders. They may give their pictures away as presents, take them home, or otherwise use them constructively. No child may destroy his work and thus obliterate his very self and his past in an attack of self-destructive rage, or as a revenge against the therapist.

In this manner a tangible record of each child's development as a painter is built up. The folders become a major tool in helping the children to become aware of themselves and of their growth. Most of the children have never experienced much continuity and quiet growth. Their pasts are full of painful events which they need to repress or wish to forget. They are not in the habit of looking forwards and backwards. Learning through experience is impaired because memories are quickly forgotten or distorted.

Paintings are tangible substances of a person's past. The painter's mood, his preoccupations, his unconscious wishes and conflicts, his knowledge and skills, and his relationships are the substance of which pictures are made. Looking at their pictures, the boys face evidence of a past that is undistorted and unembellished. Their paintings recall their successful creative efforts to the children. They touch upon past inner experiences, recalling fantasies and wishes which may still be active or may have changed in the course of time. They also recall the material struggle with brush and paint which was part of the creative act.

Looking through their old pictures, comparing old work to recent work, can be reassuring, constructive experiences, not only for the painter, but also for the whole group as they look on, comment, and pass judgment. By helping the children to recall incidents connected with their paintings, it is often possible to deepen and reinforce the meaning of past experiences. On such informal occasions the children learn to know themselves better and also learn to know each other as they compare paintings and become aware of differences and similarities.

The children's feelings about their folders reflect their feelings about themselves and also the transference relationship to the therapist. It is subject to many ups and downs and changes with the child's development. To some children their folders represent foremost a proof of their existence. An overanxious child may come every day to make sure the folder is still there. Children who cannot accept themselves may use their folders for storing up odds and ends they have salvaged and begged from others. Many boys' feelings fluctuate between pride and destructive impulses. Some children use their folders to reassure themselves of their ability and growth. Space does not permit a more detailed analysis of the various manifestations of the children's feelings.

The process of learning is so complex and all-pervading that it would be impossible to do justice to the subject in the framework of this short study. The material presented in this chapter will be supplemented in Part III, which consists of case histories. The learning process of those boys will be described over a period of two to three years and will illuminate certain aspects of learning which were only briefly touched upon in this chapter.

ART THERAPY AND AGGRESSION

LIFE AT Wiltwyck School is colored by the prevalence of aggression. Even the boys' amiable small talk and play consists for the most part of insults, threats, profanity, and aggressive horseplay. The children's habitual response to all conflicts and adversity seems limited to aggressive acts, tantrums, and destructiveness. Because aggression is so ubiquitous and undifferentiated, it hides rather than reveals the children's personalities. It seemed, therefore, best to approach the specific problem of aggression in art therapy only after the reader had become more familiar with the children and their painting.

Aggressive Behavior

Aggressive behavior is not itself accessible to treatment by art therapy. Keeping peace and order during art sessions is chiefly a disciplinary task which the art therapist performs in order to be able to conduct the program. Aggressive behavior can be tolerated only as long as it does not seriously interfere with painting. The logic of this basic rule can be understood and accepted by the children, but they are unable to maintain peace and order without the therapist's controlling influence. It is not always easy to find a proper balance between freedom and controls. Painting is an emotionally charged activity which would not thrive under overly rigid discipline. Complete lack of controls on the other hand would quickly destroy all attempts at sublimation.

For instance, the children could not be free to attack the therapist physically or abuse her verbally beyond a certain point. Yet the creative act often arouses emotions of anger or despair. The therapist, who is so much a part of the children's production, is bound to receive her share of those feelings. Suppression of all hostility against the therapist would therefore inhibit the creative process. Or, the children's small talk is interspersed with profanity and mutual insults. To forbid all dirty talk would amount to gagging the boys, yet sexual profanity and mutual abuses have to be limited. If the mood should gather momentum, it would soon reach a pitch of sexual excitement and guilt and anger that would make sublimation impossible. The therapist who tolerates such a mood would be viewed with distrust and contempt. The permissiveness would be interpreted either as foolish weakness or as a sign that she herself enjoys the profanity, and, in either case, the children would no longer feel secure.

Just as all children, the boys of Wiltwyck need to maintain a rigid image of moral rectitude in the adult to help control their own frightening and dangerous impulses. And yet, as all children, they will try again and again to seduce the adult to give in to regression and instinctual gratification. The adult who responds by regressing to the children's level creates a disastrous and frightening emotional situation for them. The children's security depends both on the adult's acceptance and understanding of their emotional difficulties and on his capacity to help them master and control their impulses.

Although behavior problems have to be met as they arise, the therapist will strive to avoid headlong collisions with the children's tempers and hostilities. Disciplinary actions detract rather than help the therapeutic work. The therapist will concentrate on maintaining a working atmosphere where the desire to paint prevails over all other impulses. She should do her best to keep the children contented by giving help before the frustration threshold is reached, by foreseeing difficulties and imminent outbursts of temper before they occur, and so forth. When explosions cannot be avoided, she will restore order as quickly as possible. Besides its immediate practical usefulness, the therapist's handling of behavior problems is valuable in establishing her general position for the children: the art therapist is always on the side of productive work, upholding the children's creative efforts against all interference.

TRANSFORMATION OF AGGRESSION IN ART

Just as in other social accomplishments, the physical and mental energy exerted in the creation of works of art is derived both from libidinal and aggressive drives. Aggressive and sexual drives are originally undifferentiated. When aggression remains strongly sexualized, neutralization and transformation become impossible, and the prevalence of insufficiently neutralized aggressive energy distorts and hampers the creative process. According to the constellation of forces, the resulting disturbance will vary in each case. Ambition may become an obsessive need to outdo competitors. Striving for higher artistic value may turn into a compulsion for endless corrections and changes. The artist's necessary self-discipline and critical faculty may be distorted into obsessive self-debasement and self-doubt. Complete neutralization of aggressive energy is never reached. Every artist is troubled with a certain amount of neurotic doubt, compulsiveness, and emotional conflict.

The energy which the artist exerts in his labors has to be distinguished from the raw material which he forms and transforms through his work, and from the content of the finished work of art. In order to work and concentrate the artist has to be in command of his emotions. The creative act itself should therefore not be loaded with raw aggressive and libidinal energy. The artist's creations, on the other hand, remain emotionally charged and capable of evoking strong emotions in others. On a higher plane, the finished work of art still contains the primitive urges and conflicts which gave rise to the process of sublimation.

The art therapist who helps the children in their artistic production encounters derivatives of the aggressive drive as emotional content of their paintings, as destructive force that distorts and inhibits the creative process, or in transformed sublimated form as constructive energy. Often all three factors contribute to the creation of the same painting.

Channeling of Aggression

Activities requiring vigorous physical exertion lend themselves to a certain amount of simple channeling of aggressive energy. Sports, lumber work, construction work, and so forth can absorb a good deal of raw aggression. Even here the binding and channeling of aggressive energy is not as simple as it may seem. Identification with a group leader and mutual identification between members of the team is indispensible. For every task the aim has to be redirected towards a constructive goal. Libidinal and neutralized energy has to be available for the learning of skills, and high achievement can be reached only when love and interest is also devoted to the work.

The binding and transformation of aggression through art is even more complex. The simple diversion of aggression into painting of pictures with aggressive content could never be therapeutically valuable. If children were encouraged to channel their aggression into painting an aggressive picture, this would amount to an invitation to overt fantasies of sadistic revenge and would not teach them effective ways of handling emotions. Their paintings would probably have no artistic merit.

An ancedote will illustrate the point.

The Big Fist

Raymund came to the art room crying bitterly because a big boy had hit him in the mouth. Raymund was a very weak child who had no way of getting even with the aggressor. In order to console him and avoid a tantrum, the therapist suggested that Raymund paint a big fist. Thereupon Raymund stopped crying and painted a huge fist and a horrible bloody eye, with the fantasy of hitting the big boy in the eye. Since the aggressor was a much-hated bully the group commiserated with Raymund, and several boys also painted fists hitting bloody eyes. The art session deteriorated into a sadistic orgy. Even the paintings of excellent painters lost all resemblance to art. They were so vulgar and obscene that none of the boys cared to preserve his work when the mood had died down. The children's paintings were not artistically worthless because of the cruelty and aggression which they contained. Some of the "monster" pictures, for instance, expressed much deeper cruelty and more murderous fantasies. The paintings were not art because of their lack of depth and their formlessness. The boys had shared in an entirely conscious sadistic fantasy. In expressing their ideas, they had lowered their standards of achievement. Instead of sublimation there had been regression.

Raymund's most serious symptom was his masochistic need to provoke hostility, abuse and rape. He had been hit because he had invited aggression, and following his pattern he had not defended himself but had retreated nursing his injuries. Evidently art therapy could not help Raymund to resolve his emotional problem. Raymund was too weak to fight his enemy in reality. The therapist's invitation to show the big fist only emphasized his actual helplessness. Raymund's orgy of sadistic fantasies could only lead to new masochistic acts. The group's commiseration with Raymund's plight had satisfied his need for acceptance and compassion, but at the price of a collective regression to Raymund's emotional level, which made the experience therapeutically worthless or harmful.

In the incident Raymund had succeeded in seducing the therapist. In order to console the child she had catered to his neurotic symptoms. The therapeutic approach would have been to begin by calming the child and then suggesting to him that he paint a picture, not as revenge, but because he enjoyed painting. If Raymund had painted a picture after calming down, it is unlikely that it would have had direct bearing on the incident. If, however, Raymund had painted a sadistic picture in response to the incident, this would have had different emotional meaning. Raymund's painting would have expressed his own strength and comeback, not illusory strength borrowed from the therapist, and might have been more valuable for Raymund.

Raymund's story illustrates the futility of an attempt to channel aggression by consciously diverting it into symbolic action. Such an escape will lead to regression rather than to sublimation and remains therapeutically valueless.

Raymund's story is atypical. The incident probably would not have happened without the therapist's prompting. Children rarely paint pictures with aggressive content simply as substitutes for aggressive acts. A child who paints a forest fire, a sea battle, or a knife dripping with blood, is not substituting these for acts of arson, murder, and mutilation. Rather he is expressing a struggle for mastery over his destructive impulses, his fears, and guilt. This is borne out by the fact that children are usually proud of such work, expecting praise for their successful pictures, regardless of content. Unless their overtures are rejected, young children will give their bloody and gruesome pictures in all innocence as presents to beloved adults.

A boy who presents his counselor with a picture of an ornate knife dripping with blood would be telling him of his valiant and victorious struggle with his castration anxiety. The symbol of the bloody knife with its underlying identification with the aggressor indicates the child's primitive developmental level and the magnitude of his castration fear. The completed painting is a sign of the ego's victory.

Indeed, painting the picture may have been a task almost beyond the child's powers. A boy who wishes to paint a big bloody knife may find it hard even to draw his object large enough. Often the knife's handle will be too small and weak to be functional, or the blade will be drawn in wavering, indistinct outlines. Such difficulties are a sign that the child is wrestling with an abject feeling of inadequacy and insignifiance. The boy's expectation of praise and admiration for his achievement is justified at this stage of development. Since aggression and anxiety are complementary and mutually stimulating, a child's symbolic self-assertion through identification with the aggressor may well be a first step towards the binding and transformation of aggression.

THE STRUGGLE WITH AGGRESSION

A child whose ego is weak and whose superego is rudimentary and primitive is swayed by impulses which a stronger ego could easily master. Because of children's immaturity, drives are still largely undifferentiated, sexuality is aggressive, and aggression sexualized. Undifferentiated aggression is usually directed both against the self and the outside world. The child is threatened from without and within. Fear of the demonic powers of his own impulses combines with fear of retaliation, creating an emotionally and physically exhausting state of permanent preparedness for counterattack or flight. Oral and anal fixations persists. Underlying the all-pervading castration fear, earlier fears of being devoured and totally annihilated remain active. A longing for inner peace and for mastery over the demonic forces is never absent, even in the most impulse-ridden child.

Escape and Denial

Children who are particularly helpless in the face of their aggressions often seek peace by avoidance of all violent subject matter. Just because their behavior problems are so disturbing, they may be given to painting peaceful, pretty pictures of houses, trees, flowers, or stars and other designs. Such painting often remains rather sterile, since the child is denying his inner turmoil and escapes into a compulsive adherence to conventional patterns. Even so the painting may be a valuable first step towards creating something positive and may give a breathing space to the child and his environment during which relationships may be formed and deepened. Paintings of this kind contain not only the child's denial of his hostility and misdeeds, but also an appeal to take notice of his longing for a different condition, which is so far out of reach that it can be expressed only in the most conventional, impersonal form.

As a child creates for himself an island of peace and order, he may also discover latent talents that had remained hidden because of his behavior problem. Conventional subject matter may become meaningful as the child's longing for security and protection is expressed and a meager beginning may lead towards richer, more creative work. In such a development no definite line can be drawn between a more simple escape into compulsive orderliness and denial of all conflict, and reaction formations which bind and transform aggression and destructiveness more effectively and more permanently.

The Fiery Tree

Albert, an intelligent, impulsive 11 year old, spent most of his time in aimless wanderings. Although he was capable of constructive work and sustained effort, he easily reverted to destructive and self-destructive acts. He was a habitual runaway given to pilfering and vandalism. Albert was outgoing and amiable in casual contacts and elusive when relationships threatened to become emotionally charged. Albert's painting was sketchy and sporadic. He was too driven to pause long enough to complete a picture. His many sketches of the hills and trees around the school showed a keen and original perception of the world around him. Pictures of helmets, knights at arms, fencers in fencing masks, and other figures encased in protective devices expressed his need to ward off both physical danger and the emotional dangers of intimacy.

When Albert began to attempt more self-control in other areas, he developed a passion for painting little villages and country houses. There were always trees, gardens, pathways leading from house to house and many white picket fences. Everything was painted neatly and methodically. The paintings expressed Albert's longing for a peaceful, orderly world, and through painting them Albert strengthened his capacity for creating order and maintaining peace. Only one painting showed sublimation of Albert's destructive impulses. On a brilliant October day, when the hills were bright with orange and yellow leaves, Albert sketched a large tree (Plate V colorprint), faithfully observing the intricate network of the crown. Back in the art room he set out to complete his charcoal sketch in painting. He painted all branches carefully in dark brown. Then he prepared himself a tray of orange, yellow, and red colors for the foliage, with a separate brush for each color, and filled all spaces between the branches with those colors. He worked methodically but was worried whether his patience would hold out to the end. With assistance and encouragement he completed a beautiful painting. Standing against a bright blue sky, Albert's tree conveyed the feeling of autumn, when trees are aflame with orange and yellow leaves. The explosive quality of the painting was tempered by the strong organization and careful, loving execution. Albert gave his tree to the head counselor, the man who most frequently had to control Albert's destructive and delinquent acts.

Albert's art showed several methods of handling conflict. His pictures of helmets, shields, and knights expressed his attempts at isolating himself behind an impenetrable protective shell. His pretty pictures seemed in part an escape from emotional turmoil, and a denial of his aggressions. The many fences and pathways and the careful execution (which did not come easy to Albert) showed genuine attempts at controlling his impulsiveness and vagrancies and could be considered the beginning of a reaction formation. In the painting of the tree Albert obtained true sublimation. Here Albert's creative process did not differ essentially from the mature artist's methods. Moved by his perception of nature, Albert created a painting which was at once an expression of his inner situation and an inspired interpretation of reality. Albert's effort was sustained by his identification with the head counselor and by his need of his approval and forbearance.

The coexistence of mechanisms of defense, denial, reaction formation, and sublimation in Albert's art shows the mutability which makes children's art so rich in surprises. It can never be forseen when some seemingly dead end, some endless repetition, may unexpectedly bear fruit. Often a child has to go through a period of familiarizing himself with painting, or taming the seductive medium through cautious noncommital work before he is ready to express emotionally loaded material.

A development of this kind could be followed in the case history of *Matthew,* who figured largely in the section on Monsters (Figs. 14 and 15). Matthew began by painting pretty designs, flowers, and houses. At this time his aggression and hostility were expressed through diarrhea and involuntary soiling. His overt behavior was conforming and quiet. Matthew's pretty paintings were in part a denial of his condition and a refusal to assume responsibility for his symptoms. At the same time they contained an appeal to the environment to recognize his positive faculties and cultural longings in spite of his soiling. The decorative beauty which Matthew obtained constituted some measure of genuine sublimation. Later, when Matthew had overcome his soiling, he acted out his aggressions through smearing with paint. This temporarily blocked his development and led to depression and unhappiness. Finally Matthew freed himself of large quantities of anxiety and aggression through painting monsters. After that episode he obtained genuine sublimation. The cultural longings which were apparent in his earliest work could now be expressed on the basis of a sturdy self-confidence. The development might not have been possible without an initial phase of tame, guarded, defensive painting which had the approval of the therapist and where no attempts were made to force the child into expressing conflict and instinctual material before he was ready for it.

Conclusions

The mechanisms in Albert's and Matthew's development are comparable in several ways. In each boy the ego gained a foothold, by creating an island of peace within a general turmoil, through an initial denial of conflict and by building strong defenses. This can be a constructive beginning, but the development would lead to a dead end and to the impoverishment of the ego unless conflict and aggression were eventually recognized and transformed. Otherwise it might result in a personality whose intentions and ideals are high, but is helpless in the face of his impulses so that ideals and reality remain forever far apart. Albert and Matthew both found ways of expressing and sublimating much of their conflicts once they acquired the necessary inner strength.

A development of this kind need not necessarily describe a full circle from escape and denial to sublimation. Some children may use art mainly to strengthen their defenses. Such painting would never attain high artistic merit, but might still contribute to progress in other areas. Eventually an interest in crafts may fulfill the same ego strengthening functions more constructively.

Counterattack and Identification with the Aggressor

Not all children react to danger from without and within by denial and escape. Often the development leads from self-assertion by counterattack and identification with the aggressor to a genuine sense of security based on achievement. Also one must remember that both mechanisms often coexist or alternate. The two types of behavior are treated separately only in the interest of greater clarity.

The painting of many boys is often for long periods of time concerned almost exclusively with defense against castration anxiety and complementary fantasies of power and potency of a destructive aggressive nature. Snakes, sharks, battleships and rockets, swords and guns and other phallic symbols abound. The narrower choice of subject natter would be determined mostly by the constellation of forces within the individual child. For instance, whales, sharks, or wild animals often express identification with a castrating and devouring aggressor. Rockets and bombs expelling fiery matter lend themselves to expression of fear of annihilation in an explosive outburst of anal aggression, and the complementary fantasy of causing such an explosion. Octopuses or many-headed dragons may ward off castration fear by the fantasy of possessing a multitude of penises. A more crystallized Oedipus complex is often symbolized by dangerous criminals, giants, or sinister, mutilated figures like Captain Hook, one-eyed pirates, and so forth.

The evaluation of the inner meaning of children's pictures is complicated by the influence of comic book illustrations and entertainment. In cowboy or detective stories, or in stories of the various super-beings virility is equated with brute force, murder, and destruction.

Guns, knives, or magic powers of annihilation are the sole attributes of manhood. Constructive work, moral fortitude, or intelligence play very little part in those adventures. The small child's sadistic interpretation of the sexual act, his equation of the penis with a murderous weapon, is reinforced by such stories. When a child paints a picture in the comic book tradition it is not always easy to determine whether he expressed a genuine fantasy or whether he is conforming to patterns which may have little meaning or may even contradict his own feelings.

Many children paint cowboys either in the act of reaching for their guns with both hands, or shooting them off simultaneously. In many instances such a picture may express the reassuring fantasy of possessing two or more penises. At other times a child may have overcome the primitive equation between penis and dangerous weapon, and may express his ideas on a level below his own concepts, in order to conform to a traditional pattern among his peers. Sometimes a boy may even feel compelled to assume such an attitude in order to live up to the expectations of some adult who erroneously equates a forced toughness with masculinity.

The paradoxical situation may occur that a child is identified with a hero whose moral qualities are far below the boy's own morality. For example, 10 year old Leon was identified with the TV hero Gene Autry and his horse Champion. Leon was the leader of his group, and was very concerned with justice and moral rectitude. The kind of fairness and justice he maintained in the group and demanded from the counselors, his sensitive weighing of right and wrong and his ability to understand motives behind actions were far superior to anything that occurred in his hero's adventures. The transitions to a higher developmental stage is often retarded by such a primitive level of entertainment.

With increasing maturity phallic symbols should gradually lose their destructive sadistic components. Eventually the penis will cease to symbolize a destructive weapon and will instead become a highly valued possession, associated with achievement.

The corresponding transformation in art can often be observed in a gradual shifting of emphasis and in a change in style. For instance a passion for painting sharks and octopuses and bloody battles with those monsters may be transformed into an interest in the beauty of the underwater world. Paintings of airplanes dropping bombs may give way to elegant cars or to beautiful birds. Gangsters and pirates may be replaced by kings, queens, sportsmen, and other elevated personages. Religious painting may replace painting of devils and demons.

Such a development would rarely proceed in a straight line. The oscillation between identification with the aggressor and more realistic self-evaluation and self-assertion is admirably expressed in Hugo's creation of the "Pigeon Dinosaur," a black little thing half bat-half bird. At the time Hugo was just beginning to replace his belligerent behavior and temper tantrums with a striving for self-control and academic achievement.

Marvin

The variety of impulses and anxieties which may be expressed simultaneously can be followed in the lively and varied production of $10\frac{1}{2}$ year old Marvin. When he entered Wiltwyck Marvin seemed an intelligent, active, and highly imaginative little boy, beset by many fears. He was eager to communicate and capable of relationships.

His first painting consisted mostly of phallic symbols, such as a huge orange cobra, two large eels, a big pike in the act of swallowing a little fish, and other paintings. Marvin was elated by such pictures—evidently they well fulfilled their function of reassuring his castration fears. But there were other earlier fears which could not be reassured so easily. Many of Marvin's paintings depicted dinosaurs, sea monsters, or huge faces rising above the sea, ready to swallow some little boat, and other scenes of devouring aggression. Marvin labored over these pictures and often abandoned them half finished. Also he struggled for control over the paint. He had a way of covering large areas with brown and often his drawing was swallowed in the process so that only an unintelligible brown mess remained. Marvin showed much fortitude and comeback in struggling with his problems, and his capacity for maintaining a positive relationship with the therapist were a great help in his efforts.

The complexity of Marvin's inner situation is probably expressed most clearly in (Fig. 16) a picture of a completely green man in the act of leaping into a wild sea. The sharp fins of sharks are visible among the waves. Marvin explained that the diver was really a human who had disguised himself as a frog man in order to escape, but since it was just a disguise it would not help him and he would be eaten by the sharks and also drown, and this would be what he deserved.

Marvin's painting shows his struggle to assert his manhood by identification with aggressive phallic symbols. It also shows his fears of being devoured, probably as a punishment for disguising his actual helplessness with a borrowed dangerous front. But this fear is mixed with satisfaction—the false frogman is getting what he deserves, and the sharks and sea monsters are also aspects of Marvin's own devouring aggression. In other paintings Marvin's weak ego seems to be struggling against the danger of being drowned by an all-pervading surge of destructive anal impulses, and sometimes the therapist has to step in and rescue Marvin's figures from being swallowed by uncontrollable masses of paint.

Fig. 16. Size, 18 x 24 inches, tempera.

A year after his admission to the school Marvin had a sudden surge of inspired productivity during which he painted four pictures within one day. The first painting depicted two small speckled trout in the act of jumping a rapid. This picture was abandoned because, "The trout were too small to paint." Then followed (Fig. 17) a painting of a Negro man in bathing trunks with a frogmask running full speed into the sea, which is breaking in high waves at the shore. He is triumphantly holding a fish on a line. Although the waves are high, there is no doubt of the man's security and superiority both to the fish and to the sea. This was followed by a picture of Christ rising to Heaven. Christ's figure is small and still close to the ground. High above him the clouds are opening, and an angel is playing on the harp. The fourth picture shows two fighting moose of equal size on a mountain.

Fig. 17. Size, 18 x 24 inches, tempera.

In his four paintings Marvin made several important steps. In his small trout he relinquished with some regret (the picture remains unfinished) the fantasy of unlimited ferocious powers. In his deep sea fisherman he becomes human, enjoying a realistic power to swim in high water and to catch fish without fear of retaliation and death. Jesus rising from the grave shows magic confined to religious subject and to the powers of goodness. The two fighting moose are a realistic expression of masculine competition without excessive destructiveness or sadism.

In each picture there is much movement and vitality but the execution remains sketchy. This may have been due in part to Marvin's elation and excitement which permitted no pausing for careful execution. Also Marvin might not have been able to sustain his newly-won powers throughout a long-drawn-out painting. Marvin's surge of creative inspiration was a promise of things to come. A period of oscillation between earlier patterns and new concepts had to follow before his maturity could be firmly established.

Projection of Aggression

Transformation and sublimation of aggression becomes especially difficult when a child avoids painful conflict with his own aggressions by projecting them onto the outside world. Inner tension is then replaced by a continuous struggle with the environment. There exists a constant need for vigilance and self-defense which impoverishes the child's emotional life, distorts reality perception, and impairs the capacity for relationships. Since conflict is internalized only in part, the process of sublimation remains incomplete. The case histories of two unusually gifted and intelligent boys illustrates this point. In a different way each boy failed to fulfill his innate potentialities because sublimation was possible only in certain limited areas.

Theodore, Caricaturist and Illustrator

Theodore came to Wiltwyck at the age of 12. He was a detached, intelligent child who formed no strong attachments at the school. He had never been delinquent and never got into serious troubles at Wiltwyck. Yet he indulged in an underhanded, malicious kind of gossiping which created an atmosphere of mutual distrust and hostility in the group. He openly showed contempt for the ignorance and lack of intelligence of his schoolmates. His evil tongue and conceit made him disliked both by adults and children, but is imaginative story telling, his talent for drawing and painting, and his reading ability gave him status among his peers.

Theodore was an excellent draftsman, although a mediocre colorist. He drew and painted much like an illustrator of comic-book adventure stories. His work had neither the naive directness of childhood, nor was there any first-hand observation of nature. But he had an uncanny ability to pick up the technical tricks of the adult illustrator. On a superficial level his painting seemed mature for his age.

Theodore painted pictures of most of the popular heroes of boys' literature, such as cowboys, holdup men, gangsters, and detectives. He delighted in painting horrors, such as witches, mad scientists, and so forth. Theodore's masterpiece of horrors was a painting of a dead body coming to life (Fig. 18). It shows head and torso of an emaciated man in a torn blue shirt in a cave. His face has a greenish-gray color. His eyes are a decomposed mass of yellow pus and red blood. Blood is dripping from his open mouth. His bare neck and arms are a purplish-pink, and the flesh also seems in a state of decomposition. The rents in the man's garments reveal more bloody matter. The cave is painted in black, grey, purple, mustard color and sickly green. Bloody stalagmites are hanging from the ceiling of the cave. Also there are red spiders webs in the corners, and one spider web is attached to the man's raised hand. The painting is over-

Fig. 18. Size, 24 x 36 inches, tempera.

laden with detail, full of fussy, confused lines. The composition lacks a focal point. Colors are sour and muddy. There is a singular absence of formal beauty. In spite of a multitude of horrible details, the painting fails to inspire compassion or fear. Instead the spectator feels revolted and disgusted.

Theodore was well aware of the fact that his picture was horrible. He took a ghoulish pleasure in adding more and more gruesome details. He was delighted to see his audience shocked and revolted by his creation.

The fact that Theodore's painting expresses a cruel and aggressive fantasy does not in itself account for the absence of formal beauty or emotional depth in his horror painting.

In the section on Monsters many paintings are reproduced which contain as much cruelty and aggression as Theodore's dead body. Yet the paintings are redeemed by formal beauty and depth of feeling. In spite of an initial feeling of shock, it remains possible to empathize with the state of mind which compelled the child to paint his monsters. In each painting the child gives symbolic expression to deep conflicting feelings. Painting constitutes not a simple gratification of aggressive impulses but an attempt at mastering conflict.

Theodore's painting is not an expression of inner conflict. Rather it expresses Theodore's conflict with the outside world. Theodore's horrors are cruel caricatures of human beings on whom he feels free to vent his aggression.

We can conjecture that Theodore has avoided conflict with his inner aggressions by projecting them onto the outside world. This mechanism brought certain advantages. Theodore was free to develop many valuable skills, undisturbed by inner conflict. At 12 years of age he was a peaceful, neat child and a good student. He was an excellent craftsman, and had learned to draw and paint with a certain facile virtuosity. But the aggression which Theodore had projected was no longer available for transformation and sublimation. Instead the rejected emotions returned to haunt him from outside. Like the boy in Hans Christian Anderson's fairy tale of the Snow Queen, Theodore's vision was distorted so that the evil and repulsive aspects of life seemed magnified and alone worth of recognition. Inner anxiety and guilt were replaced by a fear of attacks from outside. A constant need to prove that it was not Theodore who was hostile, but that the others were attacking him, dominated his life. His rejected aggressive impulses continued to strive for gratification.

Theodore's painting fulfilled both needs. His caricatures proved how horrible and evil the world really was, while they gratified Theodore's need to inflict death and decay on his enemies. His ghoulish pleasure in painting horrors and his delight at seeing the audience react with revulsion and shock were signs of this twofold gratification. In Theodore's art, aggression was not only the theme and content of his painting, but the act of painting was also charged with sexualized aggressive energy. Painting served direct instinctual gratification and sublimation was therefore incomplete. Aggression was channeled into acting out within socially acceptable boundaries, but the road towards genuine sublimation was blocked.

If Theodore had been more immature or less talented his painting would probably have reverted to simple messing. Instead there was a one-sided development of technical skill without a corresponding emotional growth. In spite of his talent Theodore's painting failed to become art.

Painting cruel and gruesome caricatures necessarily evokes some measure of guilt. Theodore's excessive dependency on comic books may have been partly caused by a need to find reassurance in a form of art which is filled with a kindred spirit.

No basic change occurred during Theodore's 1½ years at the school. To the end Theodore remained equally removed from his inner experiences and from the direct perception of nature. With increasing success and a greater feeling of security, Theodore's need for painting horrors receded before fantasies of wealth and power. Paintings of well-dressed crooks and criminals alternated with pictures of generals, presidents, and other official dignitaries. Those paintings were clearer in form and color. Sublimation seemed more successful. But the paintings remained bound to a conventional style and failed to carry much conviction. Although Theodore was able to establish ego ideals, their fulfillment seemed out of reach for his impoverished personality. In spite of his deficiencies as an artist, his facility as a draftsman sufficed to give Theodore much prestige. His success helped him to maintain a precarious inner balance. In view of this fact, no attempts were made to devaluate his accomplishment for him, or to lead him to a recognition of his deficiencies as an artist.

Building Fences around a Disturbance

Walter, who figures in the section on Prisoners (Plate II) and later reappears in the chapter on The Learning Process, was a gifted and intelligent child. His grandiose fabrications, suspiciousness, and a constant preparedness for counterattack gave proof of his need to project his feelings and conflicts onto the outside world. Walter had many of the characteristics of a classical tyrant. From the age of 12 on, he made a practice of making pets of little boys whom he protected and spoiled. He also always had a pet hate, some unfortunate little boy whom he persecuted relentlessly. Like many tyrants Walter had a disarming charm and warmth, and a strong sense of justice which operated as long as he was in a rational mood. When Walter was upset, justice gave way to arbitrary irrational behavior.

Walter was a passionate painter with a good measure of innate talent. His painting consisted mainly of a large assortment of heroes, both good and bad, and of scenes of violence and adventure. He oscillated between identification with the aggressor or a more mature identification with positive ego ideals, which he could never maintain for long. Painting was accompanied by intense fantasizing. Walter easily became overexcited while painting, and often destroyed his pictures in a sudden rage.

For instance, when Walter painted an Indian with raised tomahawk he suddenly began to attack the painting violently. This in itself is not an unusual occurrence. Children often vent their anger on their own pictures, but usually they will use discarded or spoiled pictures, and reality and fantasy remain clearly separated. In Walter's case one received the impression that the dangerous figure which he had created and with whom he was identified had suddenly turned against him. It seemed as if Walter's creation had gained some measure of independent life to him and that he destroyed it in acute panic.

Not all of Walter's outbursts of destructiveness were clearly motivated. Often only a mounting excitement could be perceived. Such excitement was often connected with the use of color. Figure 19 shows a characteristic development of this kind. Walter had drawn a picture of two sword fighters. As long as he was meticulously coloring his two persons Walter was in control of his emotions. Later Walter painted the grass in rhythmic brushstrokes which greatly enhanced the artistic quality of his painting. In the act his excitement began to mount. When he reached the sky, Walter's excitement was barely controllable, and his wild scribbling threatened to engulf his two figures. To avoid damage the therapist had to step

Fig. 19. Size, 12 x 18 inches, tempera.

in and terminate the painting. Often paintings could not be rescued in this manner, and once a picture was destroyed, Walter's fury knew no bounds. He then was dominated by a need to revenge himself for his failure. He needed to punish the brush, the paint, his pictures, the art room, and everybody around him. Many art sessions terminated with a struggle over Walter's folder, which the art therapist had to rescue from destruction.

Such a surge of destructive fury was not a simple regression in which the boy enjoyed an orgy of aggressive acting out which started with his own painting and then gathered momentum. The destruction of his work was painful for Walter. When he saw his beloved painting disfigured, he reacted to the destruction as to an attack from the outside. It was not Walter who had done the damage, but the brush who had failed to obey, the table who had bewitched him, some hostile force against which he had to defend himself by indiscriminate counterattack. After a tantrum had subsided it was often possible to reconstruct the actual chain of events for Walter, but his insight remained on the intellectual level and was of no avail in his subsequent outbursts.

Preventive measures proved more effective. Walter could learn to anticipate an outburst and to prevent it by change of activity or withdrawal. Sometimes he would stop when he felt restless, play a game of marbles, and returned pacified and ready to resume his work. He also learned that slow, meticulous painting was an effective defense against overexcitement. His painting became more elaborate and less emotional. Walter never succeeded fully in making the transition from identification with the aggressor to identification with a positive ego ideal based on achievement and mastery of impulses. At 12 and 13 his painting still retained much unmitigated aggression. There was, however, a gradual change of emphasis from raw violence towards violence tempered by aesthetic refinement and narcissistic gratifications.

This was expressed most clearly in Walter's passion for painting portraits of bull fighters in full dress. Here murder is ritualized, and grace and elegance prevail over brute force. Walter never depicted the actual fight. He spent much time in painting elaborate embroideries, silk stockings, belts, buckles, and other trappings. The narcissistic gratification and the compulsive elements in those paintings helped bind his anxiety and aggression.

Walter also established certain taboos which limited his destructiveness during tantrums. For instance, Walter never attacked or abused women and therefore took care not to injured the therapist. Although Walter could not be reasoned with, it was possible to bargain with him and once a deal was made Walter kept his word. Slowly Walter learned to build fences around his disturbance and to protect himself and others from violent outbursts. But these fences were not reliable and the basic disturbance persisted.

Walter's intellectual capacities were relatively unimpaired. The transference to the therapist endured in spite of many ups and downs, although the relationship remained on an infantile level. The therapist was to him an all-powerful figure capable of influencing his painting in a magical way, but by and large Walter trusted in her benevolence. Walter was therefore capable of learning. In the course of 3 years he acquired much technical skill, judgment, and artistic refinement.

Walter's increasing intellectual and technical mastery did not bring about an increased emotional maturity. Painting remained bound to a primitive acting out on a fantasy level. Walter's painting was filled with infantile emotionality. Hostility, violence, narcissistic gratification, elation, and depression remained the dominant emotions.

Walter's chronic state of vigilence and preparedness against danger made it necessary for him to maintain a grandiose image of himself as of a ferocious, dangerous being. This need made realistic self-representation and self-acceptance impossible. For a child of his talent, intelligence, and creative urge, Walter's emotionality remained singularly infantile and primitive. His painting reflected the immaturity and incompleteness in his personality.

Self-destructive Behavior

The balance between pleasure in constructive experiences and joy in destructive behavior is always precarious. When aggressive acts cannot be directed against others, destructive impulses are often directed against a child's own work. As long as the painting has no great value to the child such destruction will cause no inner conflict.

When such a child vents his anger and frustration upon his own painting, he is often simply following the line of least resistance. Since aggressive acts against other children would result in retaliation and overt hostility against the therapist would be restrained, the child gratifies his destructive impulses by tearing up his work, while at the same time he punishes the therapist who has helped him to paint the picture. An inhibition against such destructive acts can be established only when the pleasure of creating begins to gain ascendance over gratification of destructive impulses. When paintings become valuable possessions their destruction is no longer a matter of little consequence.

This does not mean that destructive acts will cease once the paintings have become valuable to the child. There are many children with a gerat passion for painting who go through periods when they cannot be pleased with anything they produce. Again and again paintings are destroyed for minor imperfections, and every new beginning seems doomed to failure. The work of such children often reaches a high degree of formal beauty. The process of sublimation seems unimpaired. They become deeply absorbed in their work, and until the painting's final destruction, there is little indication of inner conflict or dissatisfaction, but all accomplishment remains fragmentary. Invariably the child feels compelled to discard or destroy his painting before it is finished. He never permits himself the pleasure of seeing his picture completed. The artist's general inclination towards self-doubt and a feeling of depression upon the completion of a work appears in exaggerated, destructive form.

Instead of a conflict between ego and id, there exists a conflict between the ego and a cruel, aggressive superego, which delights in destroying the ego's pleasures. It seems as if the superego were insensitive to the process of sublimation. It punishes sublimated and transformed gratification as severely as it would punish unmitigated instinctual gratification.

In helping a child to overcome his self-destructive tendencies, the art therapist has to avoid indiscriminate praise, since the child would then simply decide that the therapist either is insincere or lacking in judgment. Rather she confronts the child with a more rational benevolent form of criticism. Against the child's archaic and sadistic superego she sets the example of an ideal superego which recognizes the value of the ego's labors and rewards them with love and approval. Also the therapist will try to help the child directly whenever there is a rational cause for discontent with his work. Often a child will spare a painting which he has completed in collaboration with the therapist. Also it is at times possible to persuade the child to give his unfinished paintings to the therapist for safekeeping instead of tearing them up. Whenever possible the therapist strengthens the child's ego in his battle with a sadistic and hostile superego.

Attempts of this kind are seldom immediately effective. Their ultimate success depends on the child's general development, which is beyond the reach of art therapy. The art therapist's intervention introduces alternate concepts in the child's life. When a change becomes emotionally possible, the transition may be more successful because of such previous experiences. This is borne out by the fact that children who have recently overcome a compulsion to destroy and devaluate their work often attribute the change to the therapist's teaching, even though there may have been little change in the child's actual skill and the therapist may have had very few occasions to teach the child anything. The child has made the art therapist's evaluation of his paintings his own, so that his work appears to him now much better and more valuable. This change is interpreted by the boy as the result of the therapist's teaching.

CONCLUSIONS

It is never easy to determine in which direction a child is moving at any given moment. Subject matter or emotional content of the painting alone would never serve as a criterion for evaluation. Ultimately only the analysis of the child's total situation could determine the meaning of each particular painting. In the absence of such total information the most valuable clue for evaluation remains the child's mood during sessions, his approach to the medium, and the formal quality of his work.

In observing the mood one has to distinguish between the joy and elation which accompany a successful creative act, and the mad gaiety and abandon which may accompany a loss of inhibitions; the irritability and hostility of regression, and the kind of nervousness and despair which often accompany an important step forward against strong inner resistance.

There is a difference between destructive regression and the loss of emotional gains, and the kind of controlled regression which occurs when a child has to recapture some repressed stage of development in order to free himself from fixations and inhibitions. (Matthew's story is a good example of such a regression.) The inner meaning of cruel or ferocious painting will be different when the painter seems serene and at peace, or when he seems full of ghoulish enjoyment of his sadistic fantasies. (Theodore's story is an example of this kind of enjoyment.)

The formal quality of children's work will differ when the painting expresses genuine feeling or when there is pretense or hypocracy. Fixation or emotional deadlocks will result in overloaded and repetitious work, which becomes increasingly unbeautiful and sterile.

Therapeutic intervention depends on so many imponderables that it seems futile to attempt formulating any rules. In general the therapist will endeavor to accelerate the child's progress, and to overcome the inertia which is part of the resistance against all change, while leaving most of the initiative to the children. In the final analysis only the child himself can guide us towards the right path for helping him to overcome his difficulties and fulfill his potentials.

PART III

TWO CASE HISTORIES

FRANK

FRANK, a Protestant Negro boy, 9 years 8 months of age, was admitted to Wiltwyck upon petition by a home for dependent children. When Frank had been 7 years old and his brother Robert a little over 5, their mother had deserted her husband and two sons. After a short period of trying to care for the two boys at home, their father had placed them in the children's home where they remained until Frank's admission to Wiltwyck 20 months later.

The mother's desertion had been the final result of years of marital discord. The marriage had never been happy. The husband accused the wife of being an incompetent homemaker and a flirt, while the wife accused the husband of alcoholism, unfaithfulness, and lack of mental balance. The mother had frequently threatened desertion, and both children had witnessed incessant quarrels between their parents. Frank, as the older one, was soon compelled to take sides. It seemed that the father felt little compunction in using his son as a tool in his battles with his wife.

After placement at the children's home, both parents maintained contact with the boys, but visits were brief and perfunctory. Bringing gifts and candy replaced emotional support. The children's home was not equipped to give more than custodial care. During nearly 2 years of institutional existence both children developed increasingly serious behavior problems which finally led to petition for placement in a treatment home.

Under the stress of desertion and neglect, the two boys had developed opposite character traits. Robert, the younger, had become a clinging child, seeking affection indiscriminately from any adult who seemed at all inclined to fulfill his needs. His hostilities were expressed in teasing and infantile behavior. Frank, on the other hand, had become aloof, suspicious, and belligerent. Since Robert's need for maternal care could not be fulfilled in an institutional setting, it was decided to seek placement in a foster home for Robert. Frank, who seemed unable to tolerate the intimacy of a family setting, was admitted to Wiltwyck School. The separation of the brothers was not an ideal solution but no alternative seemed possible under the circumstances.

Frank was a light-skinned Negro boy, small for his age, but agile and wiry. He stuttered badly, was nervous and aggressive but able to hold his own among his peers. He was a non-reader and disliked school, although his intellectual potentialities seemed above average. He showed great aptitude for arts and crafts.

During his first 6 months of art therapy Frank was an unusually independent worker who produced easily and created no serious discipline problem. His bold and beautiful painting brought him much recognition from children and adults. He painted his first important picture 3 months after admission. He was then almost 10 years old. Frank and his classmates had recently heard the story of Odysseus and his adventures in the cave of the Cyclops Polyphemus. Frank was working outdoors when he perceived his own shadow upon his paper. He called the art therapist excitedly and asked her to trace his shadow for him. He used the resulting shape as a basis for a picture of a one-eyed monster with a pink face and large white teeth, dressed in a green suit, who held both clenched fists raised to above his head.

Frank was inordinately proud of his work. He could not wait to see it on exhibit in the dining room. It took many months before he was ready to have it taken down to make a place for a new painting. Until his discharge Frank often spoke of the painting. He considered it his first good picture and always mentioned with pride that he had been the only boy who ever thought of painting the Cyclops. When a child invests a painting with such long-lasting significance one can be certain that the picture embodies his innermost feelings of himself and the world. Since Frank was not analyzed it remains impossible to determine with certainty what exactly the Cyclops meant to him. Certain features are sufficiently prominent to permit a number of conjectures.

The story of Cyclops dramatizes archaic concepts and fears. The prominent features belong to the image of the cannibalistic, devouring mother, but attributes of the castrating male are incorporated in the story. An important feature of the story is the Cyclops' isolation which makes it possible for Odysseus and his men to render him impotent and helpless by driving a stick through his single eye.

It is not possible to determine just which features of the story were particularly meaningful to Frank, nor how much of his own fantasies were added in his painting. The fact that he emphasized the single eye and gave the monster prominent teeth and long hair seems to indicate that the archaic oral component played an important part in the underlying fantasy. Although much remains uncertain, we may conclude that Frank conceived himself as a unique, isolated, monstrous being of ambiguous sex. Frank's forced independence, his shrinking from human contact, and his deep isolation correspond to this concept of himself. His positive, constructive mood during the art session and his pride and joy in the painting indicates that the picture of the Cyclops constituted a victory over the anxieties and fears contained in the fantasies. The fact that Frank remembered the painting so faithfully indicates that his concepts remained active to some degree. On the other hand, there were no replicas of the Cyclops and no new monster paintings.

Frank's profile of an Indian chief (Plate VI colorprint) was painted a few weeks after the Cyclops. The painting is a large, impressive piece of work. The contour of the profile is drawn with tremendous power and determination. The Indian's large white teeth, bright blue eye, and war paint combine to give him a ferocious expression. Hair and headdress form a magnificent, colorful edifice. The Indian's red shirt, reddish-brown skin color, and the dark red tepee in the upper left corner contrast with the yellow-green background and greenish-yellow feathers, so that the complementary colors of red and green dominate the color composition. The Indian's round, protruding chest and his long black hair add a feminine element to the painting.

Soon after the Indian chief Frank adopted the frontal position in most of his paintings. He painted a wide array of heroes, such as Indians, cowboys, mounted policemen, etc. They were over-life-sized, stiff figures. Their features were immobile and precisely drawn. Their wide-eyed gaze bypassed the spectator and seemed to focus on a distant horizon. The mouth was tightly closed, and lips were drawn with great precision and care. All heroes were well equipped with huge highly decorated weapons and dressed elaborately. They were never represented in an aggressive act. Colors were bright and solid. Combinations of green and red predominated.

The serenity and power of Frank's heroes contrasted with his behavior in daily life. Frank seemed at this time particularly insecure, provocative, and belligerent. A beginning of transference to the art therapist brought about increasing demandingness and dependency. The beginning of each art session was now marked by Frank's clamoring for attention. He could not settle down to any work, nor could he permit anybody else to work undisturbed until the therapist had given him her undivided attention long enough to start him off on his painting. Once he became engrossed in his work Frank was pacified. When he completed one of his huge heroes Frank seemed happy. His belligerence abated and even the stuttering lessened. Frank's huge heroes seemed a compensation for his shortness and helplessness. The fact that he was able to paint pictures which conveyed a genuine feeling of strength proved that he was able to mobilize considerable inner resources in the creative act.

During his first 6 months at the school, Frank's mother visited frequently. The father came only once. He made great promises of gifts, money, and frequent visits, and assured the boy that he would soon establish a new home for him and his brother. Soon after the visit the father disappeared, and for the next year Frank received no gifts or news from him. During his first half year at the school, Frank maintained absolute solidarity with the father. He could not forgive the mother's desertion and was convinced of her guilt in the discord which preceded her departure. He implicitly believed in his father's grandiose fabrications. When Frank learned that his younger brother was now living with the maternal grandmother, his hostility against mother and brother increased.

In the face of Frank's hostility and rejection his mother did not cease in her efforts to win his love and trust. Upon separation from the husband she had found steady employment, and the independence she craved. She seemed now ready to take active interest in her children.

Frank's slow change of heart was in part the result of his disappointment and the father whose irresponsible behavior contrasted with his mother's continuous interest. Another important factor was Frank's growing attachment to the head counselor. In order to help Frank to overcome his resistance towards establishing any kind of relationship with his mother, the counselor often talked with Frank about her and expressed his admiration and liking for her whenever this seemed acceptable to Frank. Because Frank never kissed her, the counselor playfully threatened that he himself would kiss Frank's mother on her next visit if Frank would not take advantage of the privilege of kissing such a pretty woman. Thereupon Frank responded by kissing his mother for the first time since their separation. The counselor's attitude established for Frank the image of a family situation where both parents are at peace and where he would not lose the father's love and protection if he showed love for the mother. Also rivalry between Frank and the counselor was acted out on a playful level, and Frank was encouraged to win out against the adult rival. Thus Frank was encouraged to express his repressed love and longing for the mother, but at the same time Frank was placed in a highly seductive situation with her, and this brought about new conflicts and problems.

Frank's mother was overjoyed by the first signs of warmth and forgiveness from the son. She was from then on eager to cooperate in Frank's rehabilitation. The following 2 years were marked by Frank's conflicts and ambivalences concerning his parents and his brother. Frank's problems were essentially those which every child faces. There was the disappointment with the mother's desertion and infidelity which every little boy experiences upon the arrival of a sibling, only in Frank's case this desertion became reality when the mother later left home. There was a turning away from the mother towards the all-powerful father and identification with him, and the later deflation of the father's image. Only Frank's father supported the child's hostility to the mother and exploited it for his own needs, helped to establish an irrational image of himself and finally utterly disappointed and failed the boy. The older sibling's normal fear and jealously of the new baby who threatens to displace him in the mother's affection proved well founded since Robert was living with the grandmother while Frank had to live in an institution.

At every turn, reality proved the child's worst fears and expectations. Frank's growth showed the normal conflicts of childhood magnified and charged with almost intolerable ambivalences. Seven months after admission Frank began to see the agency's psychotherapist in regular weekly sessions. Treatment continued until Frank's discharge. Space does not permit a full presentation of Frank's development in therapy. Our study is focused on Frank's artistic production and his conflicts and growing pains will be described only as they appear in painting.

The emotional change which was set in motion by Frank when he began to re-establish relationships with the mother resulted at first in increased restlessness, provocative behavior, and testing of the therapist. Later Frank began also to be dissatisfied with his painting. Up to now Frank had painted rather like a gifted strong-willed 8 to 9 year old. His painting had the unerring certitude which belongs to early latency, when inner experiences prevail over observation of nature. Frank now declared that his paintings were babyish. His faces unreal, the proportions of his figures faulty, his lines too straight and his colors too even. He wished to draw in a more grown-up way. Instead of drawing in stiff, straight lines he wanted to draw more loosely and use "wiggly lines." Also he wished to apply shadings and color variations and give his figures more volume and more motility.

This desire seemed entirely justified in an intelligent and talented 11 year old. Indeed, Frank's painting was beginning to show signs of stagnation and was becoming increasingly meticulous, stiff and lifeless. His casual sketches were much more mature and expressive than his finished pictures. His painting was more infantile than his perception and feelings. But the realization that there were many possible ways of painting and that the choice rested with him evoked ambivalent feelings of such violence that Frank's progress became an unending series of conflicts and deadlocks.

In his attempt to find a new style Frank tore up innumerable pictures, terrorized his schoolmates, made incessant, impossible demands on the therapist, and repeatedly attempted to destroy all his paintings. Frank's painting of a magician (Fig. 20) shows a typical oscillation between two conflicting approaches. Frank began with a simple, stiff drawing and bright solid colors. He left the face blank but covered the area with a light brown. Dissatisfied with the result he set out to improve the painting in various ways. Upon the yellow-green mantle he scattered black brushstrokes, giving the impression of a leopard's skin. The red vest was enlivened by flame-like orange brushstrokes. Finally Frank spent much time painting the turban. He changed color and shape several

Fig. 20. Size, 24 x 36 inches, tempera.

times and eventually arrived at a light green color with orange-red highlights, a complementary color combination which also appears in Frank's Indian (Plate VI colorprint), and later in his Mexican (Plate VII colorprint). The face remained blank to the last. Frank tried hard to force the therapist to paint it for him but finally drew a very stiff stylized face himself. Frank was dissatisfied with the painting. He did not like the face because it was too stiff and infantile, and he did not like the shading of the magician's clothes because it was too messy and wild.

The nature of Frank's conflict was particularly clear in his difficulties in painting faces. Frank habitually left the area of the face blank to the end, and then tried to force the therapist to draw the face for him. Occasionally he drew a face in the very careful, stiff manner as represented in the magician's face. Sometimes he could not be moved to any action and the therapist had to draw the face for him. Sometimes Frank quickly and angrily drew a face just to prove to the therapist that he could not draw faces. Invariably such quick sketches were more alive, expressive, and realistic than anything which Frank produced when he laboriously tried to draw a perfect face, but those faces seemed to have an intensity of expression which Frank could not tolerate. His dilemma seemed insoluble. Anything he painted in a fluid, mobile manner seemed to him imperfect and messy, while anything painted in a meticulous and stiff style seemed infantile and babyish.

At this point Frank's folder, which was filled with paintings of his different stages, became an important factor in his struggle for integration. He repeatedly added improvements in his new manner to his favorite old paintings, or cut out heads from his old pictures and added a new body, so that past and present were fused in one painting.

Frank's conflicts persisted throughout the better part of his second year at the school. Frank's behavior during art sessions oscillated just like his painting. Mature understanding alternated with infantile magic thinking. At times Frank could learn by experience and share his problems with the therapist. At other times he was quite irrational. Often when he spoiled a picture he accusingly said to the therapist, "See what you made me do." Just like an infant for whom Mother is the cause of all misfortune that may befall him. He adopted all sorts of superstitions. Often he moved to another table when he had ruined a painting because "The place had brought him bad luck." He accused children who worked at his table of giving him a "jinx," and so forth. He tested the therapist in any possible way and used his unhappiness as a means of sadistic revenge. Yet Frank desired to continue the relationship. No matter how difficult his behavior had been, he always managed to do something constructive toward the end of the session, so that the period ended on a friendly note. Eventually Frank's acting out threatened to take precedence over painting. Fortunately the group had at the time grown tired of Frank's disruptive behavior, and a combination of group pressure and increased firmness of the therapist reduced Frank's acting out.

The turning point came when Frank re-enacted and resolved his basic conflict in a painting of a rocket ship. Frank was then 12 years old. One day he drew a simple shape of a rocket and painted it in many shades of grey. He painted the sky a darker grey. Then he added red and orange colors both to the rocket and to the sky. He loosened his outlines and applied so much color that the rocket ship was in danger of ending up in a muddy mess. Frank explained that the rocket was melting in the sun. He then decided against such an end, and with the therapist's aid changed the dark muddy sky to a blue sky and restored the outlines of the rocket ship. The end result was an interesting painting in grey and blue with orange and red highlights. Although the subject was simple the painting was not infantile, and in spite of the explosive quality of the subject, there was no chaos. Frank was inordinately proud of the picture. For once he felt that he had painted a "grown up" picture. He was delighted with the shadings and his "wiggly" lines, and felt in every way victorious and successful.

Superficially Frank's feeling of victory and pride seemed out of proportion. A rocket ship is hardly an appropriate subject for a 12 year old of Frank's talent and experience. It rather seems a regression. Indeed Frank did regress during the painting, but later regained control and created a coherent well-integrated picture out of his almost chaotic smearing. In such a situation the child's mood and behavior remain the best clues to the meaning of the regression. Throughout the session Frank remained unusually calm, concentrated, and cooperative. He felt victorious and elated by his accomplishment, and expected praise for it. His subsequent painting showed a sudden increase of freedom, emotional depth, and maturity. Frank's remarkable Mexican (Plate VII colorprint) was painted shortly after the rocket ship episode. It can be concluded that Frank's temporary regression served to remove repressions and inhibitions which were no longer necessary.

We recall that Frank's desire to paint what he termed a "grown-up picture" was inhibited on the one hand by his inability to relinquish an infantile style and on the other hand by a fear of the emotions and impulses which came to the surface during more spontaneous painting. The rocket ship episode proved to him that those impulses were no longer dangerous, but could be controlled and utilized by his more mature ego. Consequently Frank became able to give full rein to his creative capacities. Frank's attachment to his earlier style can be understood in the light of his previous experiences.

When Frank first came to the school he had recently been abandoned by both parents and left at the mercy of a cold, impersonal environment. For protection against a dangerous world and against his own desperation and violent rages, Frank had to rely solely on his inner resources. His earliest paintings were created in an effort to establish powerful, splendid figures capable of protecting him from danger from within and without. His creations combined many frightening qualities of both parents as he conceived of them. The paintings satisfied his inner needs only while he remained aloof and isolated. Once Frank began to form relationships those rigid images no longer expressed his new perception of the world. A need arose to give expression to more modulated emotions and experiences.

As Frank began to express relationships, the ambivalences of his early childhood entered the creative process. Painting no longer served as a protection against inner turmoil. Instead the creative act itself became a battlefield of conflicting forces. Integration could be reached only through a supreme creative effort.

The integration of conflicting developmental stages can be followed graphically by an analysis of Frank's Mexican (Plate VII colorprint). The painting can be divided into three sections: a bottom part which includes brown mountains, blue and brown pants and a wide brown belt. Here the painting is undifferentiated and retains infantile anal qualities. From this foundation rises a powerful torso, which occupies the center part of the painting. The body maintains symetrical bilateral balance. A vertical row of buttons serves as axis. The complementary colors of red and green create a violent contrast. The upper third of the painting expresses a different mood. Balance is not rigidly centered. There is a feeling of motion and interplay between head and background. The color composition is more modulated. A pale grey-blue background, the soft pinkish-brown face and the color of his green shirt which is enclosed by the Mexican's long black hair, and the red-brown headband form a self-contained subtle harmony of related and contrasting colors. The facial expression corresponds to the mood of the color composition. The head is lightly inclined, and the axis of the eyes tips to the left. The eyes are a little out of focus. The right one looks slightly to the upper right, the left one, straight ahead and downwards. This creates a dreamy, inwards look. The heavy eyebrow and small sensitive mouth create a moody brooding expression. The emotional impact of the painting is generated by the great tension which exists between the complex spiritual quality of the head which crowns and dominates a body that contains much violence and raw power.

If we compare the Mexican with Frank's Indian chief, we see both the distance which Frank has traveled within the short span of two years and the unchanging basic qualities of his work. The contrast between red and green, the red chest, the long black hair, and the powerful, broad style of painting remains the same. But the Indian's face repeats the aggressive power contained in his body and in the barbaric splendor of the headdress, the Mexican's face adds a spiritual dimension which is absent in Frank's earlier painting.

At this point it is interesting to compare our findings with the evaluation of a psychologist. The following is an abstract of a psychological evaluation from approximately the same period. ". . . He is highly stimulated by the emotional impact of the world around him and overpowered by emotional stimuli. Reacts either by blocking, suspiciousness, and evasion, or acts out in unmodulated explosive way, which results in anxiety. . . He perceives himself as evil, bad, unlike others. He is unsure of his reactions, and aspires to be a powerful but benign figure who can protect himself. The dangers inherent in the world around him are varied and many. Therefore he reacts in a guarded, evasive fashion, presenting as little of himself as possible to others. His concept of female figures is negative—but in many respects there are indications that he has strong identifications with female figures but pictures them in a mascuilne role . . ."

From our point of view, the psychologist's findings would apply best to Frank's painting of Cyclops. This tallies with the fact that the Cyclops was at the time still an important and meaningful memory for Frank. Frank's later paintings show his basic problems not as openly. Instead we see more of the processes by which Frank is able to transform and sublimate some of his conflicts, or incorporate them in a superstructure where they become a constructive force. However one has to remember that this positive development appears in an area here Frank had the resources of a strong inate talent.

Before continuing with a presentation of Frank's artistic development during the 6 months which followed the Mexican painting, we have to recapitulate briefly the major development in his home situation and his general development at the school. Towards the end of Frank's first year at Wiltwyck his mother began considering possibilities of re-establishing a home for her children, but finally had to face the fact that she could not possibly both earn a living and supervise two boys. Robert, who had been with the grandmother, was placed with a friend of the family who became an excellent foster mother to him. Frank frequently visited Robert on weekends.

At Wiltwyck Frank continuously acted out his family problems. His sibling rivalry colored group living and interfered with forming of friendships. Frank's ambivalence towards his mother was reflected in his relentless testing of all women at the school. There was much open hostility towards men, but also a great need for protection and moral support from strong male figures. Frank's relationship with the head counselor continued to substitute in part for the lost relationship to the father.

For a while Frank's testing took on an obsessive, perfectionist quality which threatened to become quite irrational and self-stimulating. It was possible to counteract the irrational trend by reality experiences and setting of limits. The following example is typical for this period: Frank became very fussy about his clothes. He got into a habit of tearing up or discarding clothes because of minor imperfections. Once he had informed his counselor that two buttons were missing on the sleeve of his dress coat. When it was time for a home visit Frank discovered that she had failed to replace the buttons. He thereupon stamped on his coat, slit the back with a razor, and demanded a new coat. His coat was sewn together immediately and Frank was presented with the fact that he had to accept this coat or travel in his everyday jacket. Frank never again went to the same kind of extremes in matters of clothing. Frank went through a corresponding period of obsessive perfectionism in art where he tore up innumerable paintings because of minor flaws. Group pressure and realistic, firm handling of his behavior sufficed to put an end to an increasingly irrational trend.

When Frank had been at Wiltwyck for about 2 years, his father reappeared. Frank received a baseball glove from him and later began to see him on home visits. Father was at this point ready to admit to his own shortcomings and disturbances, and would have wished to re-establish a home with his wife. Mother remained reluctant, doubting whether it would be advisable and possible to re-establish a close relationship with a disturbed man who also was a heavy drinker. Within the next 6 months the parents came to the conclusion that they both desired to care for their children but were not able to set up a home together. Consequently efforts were made to find a foster home for both boys. Eventually Robert's foster mother undertook to admit Frank in her home. Both parents agreed to share financial responsibilities. Frank was $12\frac{1}{2}$ years old when he joined his brother in the foster home. Quarrels between the parents, mutual accusations, and competing for the child's favor never ceased entirely. To date, Frank and his brother live in an atmosphere filled with tensions and family quarrels. But this part of the story no longer belongs to our study.

Frank's last half year at the school was dominated by his attempts at forming a more realistic concept of his parents and establishing ego ideals.

Frank began to participate in group activities. He became an excellent baseball player, and a sportsman ready to accept rules of fair play. He also improved academically. His art was much influenced by the fact that his mother liked drawing, so that the common interest served as a bond between them. His mother's pretty picture of ladies in evening dress and of flowers were much admired at the school. The fact that Frank's work had

Fig. 21. Size, 18 x 24 inches, brush and black tempera.

greater scope and depth than Mother's rather adolescent painting served to give him a healthy feeling of his own worth and potentialities. He began drawing women—and this helped clarify his concepts of sexual differences. He desired to become a painter, and painted and drew many pictures of painters and of a painter's tools. Figure 21 is a good example of Frank's last pictures.

There is still much emphasis on clothes. In Frank's mind, a painter would be incomplete without French beret and eccentric necktie. But the face beneath the huge beret is expressive and mature beyond Frank's $12\frac{1}{2}$ years. Frank's creative efforts to establish for himself an image of a mature painter went parallel with a greedy and obsessive accumulating of painting gear. Frank blackmailed his father into buying him an expensive set of oil paints. He collected brushes, pads, pencils, and became inseparable from his outfit. Towards the end, compulsive polishing, cleaning and rearranging of the paintbox replaced creative work. Frank seemed preoccupied with consolidating a protective outfit which would support his self-esteem in the new environment he was about to enter. Fortunately, this outfit did not mask incompetence. Frank was capable of making good use of the material which he had accumulated. He continued to paint after discharge. Art, crafts, and carpentry continue to play an important role in his life. Since the parents assumed full responsibility for the child, the agency's function ended soon after discharge.

Concluding Remarks

Frank is a child with strong inate talent for the plastic arts. Throughout his life at the school, painting remained an important factor in his development. He uses art mainly for symbolic acting out of strong ambivalent feelings. Painting is particularly important because Frank remains a somewhat isolated, aloof person whose capacity for direct communication is limited. Frank's preoccupation with his family conflict tends to limit the scope of his production. The basic emotional content of his painting never changes. At certain difficult periods of his life, Frank's ambivalences threaten to paralyze or destroy his creative ability. His obsessive compulsive defenses threaten to constrict and deaden his art. Explosive emotions tend to disrupt the process of sublimation. During many ups and downs Frank develops an increasing capacity for sublimation and integration of his conflicting feelings In his most moving paintings Frank estabishes a balance between his emotionality and a strong, well-structured form which contains and expresses the emotional content on a high level of sublimation.

GORDON

Gordon, a 9 year old Protestant Negro boy of medium-dark complexion, was admitted upon his mother's petition. The mother, whom we shall name Mrs. A., declared his behavior to be beyond her control. Gordon terrorized his younger siblings, climbed on top of cars, broke windows, and also often ran into heavy traffic, endangering his life. Mrs. A.'s disciplinary measures, which including beatings and withholding of meals, were of no avail.

Gordon was the eldest of five siblings. Besides him there were Edward, 7, Sybil, 6, and the twins, Theresa and Carol, who were almost 2 years old. Gordon's father had been separated from the family for nearly 4 years. The twins were born out of wedlock. Their putative father contributed to their support and visited them. The family of six was living in two small rooms and subsisting on public welfare.

Gordon was born in Virginia and spent the first year of his life at his grandfather's farm where both parents lived after their marriage. Gordon's mother was unable to recollect the exact length of time spent at the farm. It seems likely that he frequently stayed there until the family moved to Chicago when he was 5 years old. Gordon himself always remembered the farm in a rosy light. He described it as a primitive but idyllic place with lots of open space and many animals, including several horses.

The carefree rural life ceased when the family moved to Chicago and later to New York. There came several years of wandering and insecurity when Gordon was boarded with friends and relatives most of the time. The father soon left the family. During the last year and a half the mother had attempted to maintain a home for her children, but at the time of Gordon's admission to Wiltwyck Mrs. A. felt unable to cope with her large family and was actively seeking placement for all her children.

Mrs. A. was a tall good-looking woman with much personal charm. She was well dressed and groomed. Although she seemed under great emotional strain, Mrs. A. maintained perfect outward calm and poise during her interview with the social worker.

Mrs. A. described Gordon as having been a healthy baby up to the seventh month when he had slight convulsions. He had feeding difficulties at a later age. Since Gordon had been boarded out so much, the onset of his behavior difficulties could not be determined. Mrs. A. related that Gordon had run in front of a car when he was 8 years old and had suffered a broken leg. He was hospitalized for many months, was disturbed and hyperactive at the hospital and had to be tied to his bed on several occasions.

Mrs. A. described her husband as an unstable personality who drank heavily, was very suspicious of her, and at times violent. He was a skilled house painter, but often out of work because he could not get along with his employers because of his extreme perfectionism.

Gordon was admitted to Wiltwyck with a tentative diagnosis of behavior disorder. Soon after his admission Mrs. A. succeeded in placing Edward and Sybil in a home for dependent children, and the twins were taken into their paternal grandfather's home. When Mrs. A. had succeeded in finding shelter for all her children, she suffered a nervous breakdown and was admitted to the mental ward of a city hospital suffering from depression.

Gordon learned of his mother's hospitalization 2 months after his admission to Wiltwyck when he received a postcard from her. For the next 4 months Gordon had no sign of life from anybody. His family was dispersed and his ideas of the whereabouts of his siblings were vague. He suffered intensely from the isolation and uncertainty of his situation.

Gordon's social worker made many attempts at establishing communication with Mrs. A. via the hospital. He was informed by Mrs. A.'s social worker that her condition was improving and also that she had been writing to Gordon regularly once a week. However none of those letters ever reached Wiltwyck, and it was impossible to ascertain just what had happened to them. Four months after the first postcard, Gordon received a letter from the mother. This time she related that she was about to be discharged from the hospital and promised him a visit in the near future. Then again Gordon was left without further news. Mrs. A. had left the hospital without giving a forwarding address. Later it was found that she had entered another hospital, this time for a surgical operation. After her recovery she finally approached the agency herself. She seemed much improved and more able to cope with the complexities of her life. She related that she was receiving psychotherapy as an outpatient of her first hospital.

Mrs. A. had no desire for a reunion with her children at this point. Instead she entered a training school for nurses, from which she graduated 2 years later as a practical nurse. Mrs. A. seemed unable to maintain a motherly relationship to all her children. Gordon was the only one for whom she retained a strong attachment. Although she was unable to establish a warm, motherly relationship even with Gordon she did her best to do right by him within the limitations of her own disturbance. She maintained contact with the agency, cooperated in planning week-end visits, and accepted guidance in the handling of Gordon's problems.

When Gordon first entered Wiltwyck he was a small child with handsome, delicate features. His looks were marred by protruding teeth, a condition that seemed caused or aggravated by excessive thumb-sucking. Gordon sucked his right thumb and simultaneously twiddled the top of his right ear so that his hands were crossed as if he were hugging himself. He was neat and clean, particular about his clothes, and quite aware of his good looks. He was shy of physical contact and recoiled before demonstrative affectionate behavior either from men or women.

Gordon was placed among a living group of young children and adjusted surprisingly well to the living situation. He formed no friendship with any child, but he got along fairly well with everybody. Except for a few isolated incidents of sex play Gordon kept aloof from sexual play among the boys. The destructive delinquent behavior which he had shown at home subsided quickly at the school. There was never any stealing or wanton destruction of property. Gordon's temper tantrums, on the other hand, continued, and Gordon was capable of dangerous aggressive acts in a tantrum or even in a burst of sudden anger.

Gordon's adjustment in the academic school was less satisfactory. Although Gordon was at least of average intelligence, with indications of high average to superior endowment, he seemed unteachable. He had arrived as a non-reader and was unable and unwilling to learn to read and almost equally reluctant towards arithmetic. He was easily frustrated and defiant and hostile to teachers. Temper tantrums occurred frequently during school hours. Gordon also disliked sports and games. The only part of the school's curriculum which he enjoyed was carpentry. crafts, and, most of all, art. Because of his inability to learn in other areas, Gordon was permitted to spend much additional time in the shop and the art room.

Gordon's emotional life seemed exclusively centered around his mother and siblings. He anxiously waited for news from her and immediately answered her infrequent letters. Everything he produced in arts and crafts was destined as a present for her. He also showed concern over the fate of the twins who were his favorites. He saw the breaking up of his family as a result of his mother's illness and held fast to the belief that the family would be reunited soon after her discharge from the hospital. He fantasized of moving into a large house in New York or Chicago or, better still, of the family's return to the grandfather's farm. Up to the time of his discharge Gordon never entirely relinquished his hopes for such a reunion.

Gordon showed a great affinity for art from the beginning. During the first 6 months his painting was somewhat stiff and overcontrolled. He worked slowly with much regard for detail. Occasionally it took him 2 weeks or more to finish a painting. This cautious, careful work was not motivated by a need to be good or to please the therapist. Rather, Gordon's treatment of his paintings seemed to be part of a strong narcissism. Gordon treated his paintings as extensions of his person, and just as he desired everything else that belonged to him to be of excellent quality and elegance, he desired his paintings to be perfect. Gordon's creative capacities and manual skill were fortunately adequate for his standards of perfection, and Gordon was as a rule proud and delighted with his work. Gordon's subject matter showed his isolation. Usually there was just one small animal or person in the middle of a lonesome landscape. Exceptions were several paintings of army life which seemed related to Gordon's traumatic experience of accident and hospitalization. He spent several sessions on a picture of a soldier being carried on a stretcher, with tanks in the background. All army pictures were painted in many shades of brown.

The Eskimo (Fig. 22) was painted four months after Gordon's admission. It is a strong and moving picture of utter solitude and isolation. The Eskimo, dressed in brown suit with white fur trimming and green shoes is standing stiffly in the middle of the picture. He is surrounded by white snow. At shoulder height the plain rises in two cone-shaped white mountains reminiscent of breasts. The sky is a strong blue, thick white clouds of various shapes and sizes are distributed with a feeling for complex rhythmic balance. The Eskimo's face, surrounded by white fur, stands out in the exact center between the two mountain peaks. The Eskimo is carrying a spear. His only companion is a black dog harnessed to a sled.

We recall that Gordon was at the time without news from his mother. The painting expresses the child's longing for her. He places himself between her breasts—the mother's coldness—the mountains are of snow—his heroic

Fig. 22. Size, 18 x 24 inches, tempera.

determination at survival in a cold and strange surrounding—the Eskimo is well equipped for the climate, possesses a faithful dog, a sled, and a trusty spear. It also expresses a state of waiting expectancy which paralyzes action. The Eskimo is standing immobile, all life seems centered in his large dark eyes. The light green shoes add a frivolous touch to the tragic painting and recall Gordon's strong narcissism. Up to his discharge more than 4 years later Gordon never quite relinquished the attitude of dogged expectant waiting which the Eskimo expressed so dramatically.

Gordon's next painting (Fig. 23) 2 months later shows a more belligerent assertive attitude. A Negro and a white man are fighting in front of a castle. The white man on the right is defending the red drawbridge which leads into the castle. He is being attacked by a Negro. The ground beneath the fighters' feet is a dark solid brown with a few tufts of grass growing in the middle. The water of the moat is dark blue; the castle walls, a yellow ocher. Gordon worked for 3 weeks on the picture. On several occasions it seemed in danger of being destroyed or discarded. Originally both fighters were white people. When Gordon finally finished the painting to his satisfaction he painted the left man's face brown, and declared that this fighter was he, himself, and that he was going to win the fight.

The sword fighters marked the onset of a very fertile period. Gordon's painting became bigger and bolder. He asserted himself by painting kings, pilots, devils, Indian chiefs, and other heroes, both good and bad. There was much emphasis on elaborate dress and ornaments which were executed with loving care and a strong sense for decorative effects. Violent action, death and destruction were not depicted. Rather there was emphasis on power, dignity, and display of wealth. The period lasted for about a year. During this time Gordon became aware of his development and growth. He looked periodically through his folder and compared his new work with his older paintings. He seemed proud of his development.

When Gordon was nearly 11 years old, his painting began to show the developmental changes typical for this

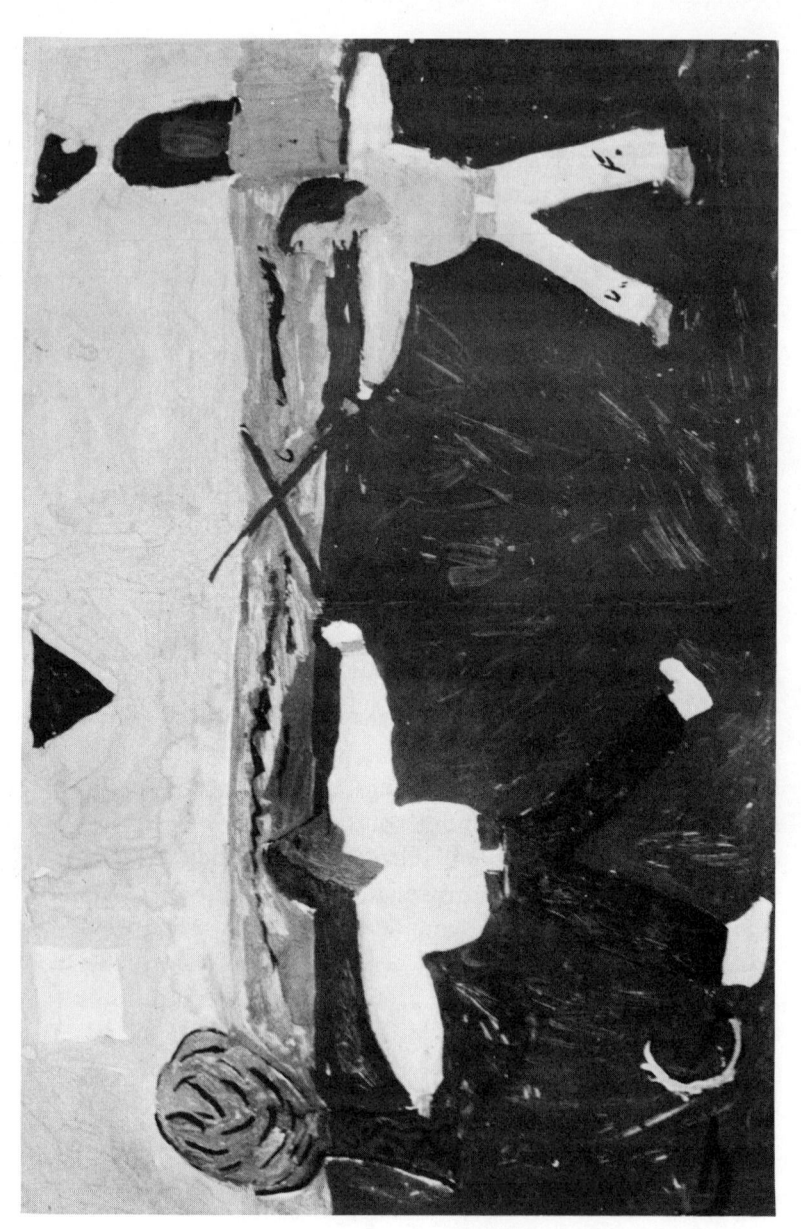

Fig. 23. Size, 24 x 36 inches, tempera.

period. His work became more realistic, his lines more fluid and mobile, and his color more varied and modulated. There was a corresponding deepening of emotional content. Complex feelings conflict and moral values are expressed. Gordon experienced the change as a victory. There was a general quickening of pace in his production, and the full extent of his creative capacities began to unfold.

Much of Gordon's work of this period centered around animals. Conflict between good and evil was often expressed in animal guise. Paintings of ferocious beasts such as lions, bears, or gorillas, alternated with idyllic paintings of horses or deer. Gordon's emotional swings usually went from evil to good and then again back to evil. *Example:* he painted a bear emerging from his cave mostly in black and grey. Then he made a quick sketch of a white village church surrounded by trees, followed by an elaborate picture of a horse's head against green meadows and blue sky. This painting was followed by a picture of a ship at sea. As Gordon painted the sea, one of his waves became increasingly large and finally swallowed and obliterated his ship. In its final form, the painting consisted of a huge menacing wave rising admidst a windswept sea. Sky and sea are painted entirely in shades of blue and grey, with white highlights. In his evil paintings Gordon created an all-pervading mood of devouring aggression and danger. His choice of color and the quality of his brushstroke were just as expressive of this mood as the bloody teeth and sharp claws of his ferocious beasts. Gordon's idyllic paintings showed him capable of creating images of a serene and peaceful world, but Gordon seemed confined to a limited number of subjects. His paintings usually depicted horses, deer, churches, or other religious subjects. When Gordon painted evil things his subject matter was wider, as if evil were rampant in a larger area of his inner world. At this time Gordon also painted his first pictures of women. His problems around this subject will be discussed later.

Gordon's increasing ambition and success in arts and crafts did not carry over into academics. Because of his failure to learn in a more conventional classroom, Gordon was placed in a classroom for children suffering from serious learning disturbances, where the boys did much project work and emphasis was placed mainly on general acceptance of the school situation. Academic learning was introduced individually as each child became ready for it. In this new situation Gordon learned to conform to classroom routines but remained unable to attempt academic learning. At 11 years of age, he still was unable to distinguish his letters or even write his full name.

Gordon's adjustment in the living situation remained satisfactory on a superficial level. Gordon continued to conform with the school's routines, did his share of housework and committed no delinquent acts. But he also formed no lasting friendships with children and adults, continued his thumb-sucking and held himself aloof from emotional commitments of any kind.

Gordon's home situation remained unsettled. His mother was completing her training as a practical nurse. His brother was living in another institution, his sister in a foster home. On Gordon's weekend visits Gordon and his mother had to stay at a friend's house. Gordon realized that no change could be expected before his mother had completed training. His hopes and dreams were focused on the near future when his mother would find a good position and would again establish a home for the family. Meanwhile Gordon was marking time at Wiltwyck. Mrs. A. supported Gordon's interpretation of his situation.

Although their plans and expectations seemed realistic on the surface Gordon and his mother's dreams of the future contained many irrational fantastic elements. Mrs. A.'s mental balance had remained precarious, her capacity for warmth and close personal contact was impaired, and her ability to cope with a complex living situation was limited. The training school provided a sheltered existance, and Mrs. A. was adequate to the intellectual demands of the training course. Once she would again be on her own she was bound to encounter new difficulties. And even though they did not consciously admit those facts, both mother and son must have been aware of the precariousness of their situation.

The task of maintaining a relationship with a mother who lacked warmth and whose responses were almost entirely on a verbal and intellectual level and the inner effort of upholding their common dreams of a better future drained Gordon's slender emotional resources to a point where he had little to spare for his daily life at the school. Gordon lived solely for his home visits. His moods and behavior at the school depended entirely on them. He was productive in those areas which helped support his self esteem and his grandiose fantasies but could not progress in any field where he might encounter failure or frustrations, or where emotional demands were made.

Gordon's progress in painting remained at the time unimpaired by his emotional withdrawal. Paintings were to him extensions of himself and the pleasure of producing before all narcissistic gratification. His inclination towards grandiose daydreams found a field where such dreams could be realized on a fantasy level. Gordon dreamt of becoming Wiltwyck's master painter, and this fantasy was less unfounded than any of his other ideas.

Gordon was developing rapidly. He learned from the painting of older children whose work he admired, and seemed confident that he would surpass them in due time.

Gordon's subject matter showed that he was establishing moral values, but those efforts seemed independent of relationships. If Gordon decided not to be delinquent, to control his temper, or to accept the moral commandments of his religion, he did this to please himself or maybe to please his family, but certainly not to please anybody at the school. Good conduct was for Gordon a matter of pride and at times a matter of expedience, but only to a small degree the result of a genuine inner change through growth and increasing maturity.

When Gordon was a little over 11 years old he began to be increasingly absorbed in the problem of painting women. His first important attempt (Fig. 24) remains a fragment. It is a full-length picture of an Egyptian princess painted on a large sheet of brown paper. Gordon explained that he got the idea from a movie wherein an Egyptian princess kills her lover. The most expressive part of the picture is the woman's face and her magnificent blue black hair which is falling in large waves over her shoulders. Her head seems bent under its weight. Her large green eyes beneath black eyebrows and heavily painted eyelids are looking straight to the left. Their gaze is focused at a distance bypassing the spectator. The woman's shoulders, torso, and arms are distinctly masculine. Her upper body is nude except for a brassière which seems incongrous on the masculine torso. The princess is wearing long white pants and over them a kind of red kilt shaped like a loincloth. In her right hand she is holding a dagger. Gordon left headdress, brassière, dagger, and sandals unpainted. He was unable to finish

Fig. 24. Size, 24 x 36 inches, tempera.

the picture, but also unwilling to throw it away. Eventually he gave it to the art therapist, a gesture which seemed to indicate that he felt unable to cope with the theme but still did not want to give it up.

Even in its unfinished state the painting remains a remarkable piece of work. Although the hair is the only part in motion, the very stillness of the figure conveys a feeling of imminent passionate violence. If we consider the conflicting feelings and concepts which the painting conveys, we cannot be surprised that Gordon was unable to complete it.

The princess has both male and female features. She is beautiful and potent in a female way (her abundant beautiful hair, her painted eyes, her adornments). At the same time she has a masculine build, carries male symbols (a knife and a cobra headdress) and wears a red loincloth in the shape of a penis. The painting shows fascination with woman and fear of woman. There is the desire to penetrate her clothes and find her secret, and the need to deny her lack of penis and to overcompensate for it by abundant adornments. There is also a fear of castration or murder as a punishment for sexual curiosity and desires.

From then on Gordon painted women off and on. The problem increased in intensity throughout his twelfth year. Gordon's greatest difficult remained drawing women's bodies. Again and again he drew masculine shoulders and torsos and seemed unable to draw a woman's breasts. Often he began by painting a woman and later changed the picture into a man. Gordon's feelings also oscillated between a desire to elevate and worship women and the impulse to abuse and degrade them.

Gordon's painting of Moby Dick, the White Whale (Fig. 25), expresses the degraded aspects of Gordon's sexuality. Gordon was then nearly 12 years old. The

Fig. 25. Size, 18 x 44 inches, tempera.

whale was painted while Gordon and a schoolmate were indulging in a playful orgy of mutual insults or "slipping." Each child accused the other boy's mother and grandmother of every conceivable and inconceivable sexual promiscuity and perversion. Both boys derived hilarious pleasure from their inventions. The boys were also playing on the double meaning of the word "Dick." Under the circumstances one might have expected Gordon to produce an overtly obscene painting, but Gordon's whale is far from crude obscenity.

The white whale is floating on the surface of a light blue sea and is spouting a blue jet of water. The sky is indicated by loose, light blue brushstrokes on the white paper, and the whale's body is painted in subtle shades of light grey with dark grey accents. The bright and silvery atmosphere of the painting contrasts with the evil expression of the whale's face. His mouth is open in a crooked kind of sneer baring white teeth and the red cavity of his mouth. There is a sly and evil look in his small black eye. The round hind flippers with a black shadow between them suggest a woman's thighs and vulva. The whole body conveys a feeling of nakedness. The whale seems a composite of all the dangerous and evil sexual fantasies that haunt the growing boy.

Gordon knew only a crude comic book version of Melville's masterpiece. With the intuition of the true artist he recreated the original poetic meaning of the tale. The incident is a measure of the depth and power of Gordon's artistic capacities. Even while he is superficially engaged in verbal obscenities he communicates in his painting those fears and conflicts which lie hidden beneath the children's ritualized mutual abuses.

Soon after Moby Dick, Gordon finally painted a woman to his satisfaction. It was an almost life-sized ¾ profile showing head and shoulders only. Gordon began the picture with the determination to succeed. He reminded the art therapist of her promise to stand by him when he painted his next woman. (The art therapist had often offered her help when Gordon had been having difficulties painting women, but Gordon had never before been able to accept her assistance.) Now Gordon asked for help in a number of minor details, but he completed most of the picture alone. Later he tried to paint a man's head as a companion piece to the lady but failed. Still Gordon was satisfied with his picture. It was exhibited in the dining room until Gordon took it home.

The painting marked the end of a long struggle. Gordon resolved his conflicts around the mother's person by turning away from sexual fantasies. His final version shows the woman's head and shoulders while the alluring and seductive body is left out. The repression was probably brought about by the return of Gordon's father. After Mrs. A. had completed training, Mr. A. had reappeared and husband and wife were again living together. Gordon's inability to paint a male companion for his female head shows his conflicting feelings about the father.

Gordon's suppression of sexual fantasies brought about a greater general awareness of the outside world and increased productivity in many areas. Gordon began sketching from nature, drew several remarkable likenesses of his schoolmates, and went out to sketch the campus and the animals on the farm. He painted a number of large animal pictures and shortly before the summer vacation he painted a Scotchman in shirt and kilt of which he was exceedingly proud. The painting indicates his persistent confusion about the sexual roles.

At the same time Gordon's relationship to the art therapist became more meaningful. Although he never identified with her person, or showed warmth and affection for her, he increasingly identified with her profession. He admired her skill and trusted in her good will towards him and his artistic aspirations. He imitated her by making himself into her assistant art teacher who helped the other boys and gave advice. He observed how the therapist evaluated each child's work according to his talent, age, and experience, and tried to understand and accept her teaching methods.

Gordon also finally learned to write his full name and delighted in signing his paintings in ornate handwriting. Upon his own request he began to see the remedial reading teacher in regular sessions. Here it soon became apparent that Gordon's reading block amounted to a deep-seated inhibition. His progress was exceedingly slow. He could not tolerate making mistakes, nor could he accept the teacher's help. His extreme narcissism and perfectionism created an almost insurmountable obstacle to learning.

We have already mentioned that Gordon's home situation changed when he was about 12 years old. After completing her training Mrs. A. did not immediately seek employment as a nurse. Instead she worked at a dry cleaning establishment and supported herself and her husband on her salary. The couple lived in a small furnished room. On home visits Gordon shared his parents' single room. There was, however, much talk about finding a larger apartment and better employment and both parents supported Gordon's fantasies of a future when he would be living with them in comfort and wealth. Whatever Gordon's misgivings about the father's person might have been, the fact that the family was re-established and that the parents were looking for a better place to live sufficed at the time to give Gordon a more hopeful outlook on life. His increased productivity, his willingness to learn, and his cautious attempts at establishing relationships were in part a result of the change in his home situation.

During Gordon's thirteenth year it became clear that his parents were too disturbed to establish a home for him. Mrs. A. eventually found a position as a practical nurse and functioned well in her profession, but the home situation deteriorated as time went on. Mr. A.'s disturbance became more serious. He seldom worked, drank heavily, and was suspicious and abusive to his wife. Mrs. A. frequently spoke of separation but somehow seemed unable to break the emotional tie to her husband. Eventually she had to admit to herself that she was in no position to make a home for a disturbed child of 12, and that prospects for a change were uncertain. But Mrs. A. was unable to admit this to Gordon. Rather she continued to cater to his hopes by fabrications and promises. Her husband seemed to live almost entirely in a world of grandiose fantasies and impracticable plans for a rich successful future. When Gordon visited his home he was confronted by the reality of a dirty cramped apartment, his mother's hard work, the father's alcoholism and idleness, and his parents' poverty. But he was also exposed to their dreams, pride and pretenses. Gordon never spoke of the squalor of his home situation or of his father's brutalities. Instead he returned from home visits full of tales of his parents' wealth, their plans for the future, and of his three bicycles and other valuable possessions. When pressed Gordon always admitted to his boasting and tried to pass his tales off as a joke. Still the need for telling such stories persisted.

Gordon's social worker had to represent reality and reason to the whole family. The great difficulty in helping Gordon to accept the fact that he would not be able to go home lay in the impossibility of presenting him with a definite alternative. Gordon was 12 years old. He had been at Wiltwyck for 3 years, and in another year he would be too old to continue at the school. Yet Gordon's academic retardation and precarious mental balance made it almost impossible to find placement in another institution. Placement in a foster home was out of the question since Gordon's whole emotional life centered around his own family. For a while it seemed as if a solution was near at hand. The agency was at the time planning to establish a residential home in the City. This home was intended to take care of older boys who had outgrown Wiltwyck but still needed treatment and guidance in an institutional setting. It was hoped that those plans would materialize within the next year, so that Gordon could be admitted when he was 13 years old. Such an arrangement would permit Gordon to visit frequently with his family, without being exposed to the full impact of his parents' disturbance and without having to share their squalor and the hopelessness of their lives. The arrangement would not burden Mrs. A. beyond her emotional and financial capacities and it could be hoped that she would be able to give Gordon some measure of warmth and motherly love. Case work, remedial reading, and artistic training could continue as long as necessary.

Unfortunately plans were still uncertain. It was impossible to prepare Gordon for a future which might never materialize. Case work could therefore not be focused on a definite goal. Instead efforts were made to replace Gordon's fantastic longing for an idealized mother image with a genuine relationship with the actual mother. Frequent home visits were arranged. The case worker discussed the experiences of the visits in his interviews with Mrs. A. and his session with Gordon. Gordon responded well whenever the home situation was tolerable. As long as he could hope for an ultimate reunion with the mother and as long as it seemed as if the living situation might improve Gordon could accept the *status quo*. He made efforts to progress in his reading, was productive in art and in crafts and told no boastful tales. Whenever the home situation was worse Gordon was lost. He became boastful, querulous, and unproductive, and wandered around the campus like a lost soul.

Gordon's progress in reading was much retarded by a change of teachers. His first teacher had been a highly skilled elderly woman. After her departure she was replaced by a young man who was less experienced, stricter, and more menacing to Gordon. Gordon thereupon ceased learning until he was transferred to another elderly woman teacher 6 months later.

Gordon's painting was in the process of transition from the naive creativity of childhood to the complex creative process of the adult artist and Gordon encountered the difficulties which are typical for this developmental stage. By 12 or 13 the talented child has reached a degree of technical skill and sophistication which makes painting on a childlike level easy. Old and tried forms and subject matter seem increasingly stale and empty. A more adult approach on the other hand implies the study of nature and an awareness of our cultural heritage. The child who was a master painter among his peers finds himself once more an untried novice who has everything to learn. A more adult approach to art requires maturity and cultural experiences beyond the 12 or 13 year old's reach. At this point the ideal situation for the growing artist would be entering an apprenticeship such as existed before the Industrial Revolution. Lacking a structured situation of this kind, the adolescent artist of our time usually oscillates for a long period between child-like painting and attempts at finding shortcuts to maturity by acquiring all sorts of little technical tricks. There is as a rule much imitation of adult art of dubious artistic merit. Serious study of nature and of our cultural heritage slowly replaces those inadequate methods.

Gordon's production oscillated accordingly between childlike painting executed with perfectionist technique, imitation of adult art of the magazine illustration type, and some valuable sketching from nature and experimentation with form and color.

Gordon's situation was further complicated by the fact that he had no companions. In his fourth year at Wiltwyck Gordon was the school's undisputed master painter. Only Walter, 12 years old, approached Gordon's talent and developmental stage, but even he was younger and more immature. Gordon had no competition and no inspiration from the group. All the exceptional painters whom he had admired had been discharged. His dream of being Wiltwyck's master painter had come true, but brought no satisfaction. Also the atmosphere and facilities of the art room no longer fulfilled Gordon's needs. He found the bickering, fights, and destructiveness of the younger children hard to tolerate. He was at an age when reality becomes increasingly important to the growing boy's painting, and his production was impeded by the insecurities and frustrations of his reality situation Throughout the better part of his thirteenth year, Gordon completed only a small number of paintings.

At the same time Gordon did a good deal of valuable sketching from nature. He was given a sketchbook and went around the campus sketching animals, horses, trees, and people. Figure 26 shows the observation skill and maturity which Gordon developed during this time. Gordon and a group of other advanced boys went on weekly sketching trips with the art therapist. During those excursions Gordon seemed more relaxed and outgoing. He

Fig. 26. Size, 9 x 12 inches, pencil.

tended to isolate himself from the group while sketching but expected the art therapist to visit him periodically. He probably would have liked best to go sketching just with her. This desire did not stem from a need for personal intimacy, but rather from a desire to share an artistic experience with an adult artist.

It is interesting that one of his few more personal conversations with the art therapist took place on a sketching excursion. The group had been sketching horses. On the way home Gordon questioned whether a horse could eat meat. The therapist explained that some animals are herbivorous, other carnivorous, and others, such as pigs or men, omnivorous, and that a horse's stomach was not equipped to digest meats. Gordon then developed a fantasy of tricking a horse into eating meat by hiding hamburgers among his hay. He imagined how the horse would develop a craving for meat so that it would begin to chew people's hands and arms as they fed it. From there Gordon launched into a fantasy of broiling the art therapist over an open fire until she would be all brown, crisp, and edible, and how he, Gordon, would eat her. The fantasy was related in all innocence and good humor. It was one of the very few occasions when Gordon seemed relaxed and ready to converse freely and intimately with an adult.

Shortly before the summer vacation a few weeks before his thirteenth birthday Gordon painted two remarkable pictures: a Spanish dancer (Plate VIII colorprint) and a Mexican on horseback. The Spanish dancer is obviously inspired by some illustration which Gordon may have seen in a magazine or on a calendar. The passionate, unusual treatment belongs to Gordon. The dancer is whirling about at great speed, her skirt so high that her pink panties are showing. One hand touches her rich black hair, which is also in tempestuous motion. The woman's face has a somber, passionate kind of beauty and her expression is almost frightening in its intensity. Under her fast moving feet there is a wide expanse of black ground with white highlights which emphasize her motion. The background is filled with huge four-leaf purple flowers with yellow highlights, which are distributed in an irregular pattern complementing and emphasizing the rhythm of her dance. Bands of green and orange are woven between the flowers, connecting them and adding to the general feeling of passionate action. Gordon painted the picture in less than 2 hours while he was alone in the art room.

Gordon's Mexican constitutes a kind of companion piece to the dancer. It is a full front view of a man on horseback equipped with ornate guns and spurs wearing a large embroidered hat. He is holding a long highly adorned whip. The man's face is masculine, hard, and cruel. He is riding a beautiful golden palomino, and behind him there is a background of desert sand and bristling cactus.

It is interesting that Gordon did not take the two paintings home. Instead, he gave the dancer as a present to the school's nurse, and gave the Mexican to the resident director. The material expressed concerned his mother and father so deeply that he could not present them with the paintings. Instead he gave the pictures to people who seemed well equipped to accept and safeguard such material.

The dancer, who evidently represents the mother, is engaged in a solitary passionate display. A wide expanse of black separates her from the spectator who remains inactive, fascinated, and overawed by the spectacle. The huge purple flowers and green and yellow streamers seem to be hurled into wild motion and anything or anybody approaching her seems destined to be caught in the mad, vortex of her dance. The mother appears to the 13 year old as a fascinating, alluring figure absorbed in her own passions, who remains forever out of reach. In his painting Gordon expresses his feelings with artistic virtuosity, intensity, and depth beyond his years.

The Mexican on horseback, which was painted at the same period, is unfortunately not available for reproduction. The painting was less original. Gordon had often painted similar subjects and the particular version adds no new dimension to the theme. There is a striking difference between rider and horse. The rider, bristling with spurs, guns, and a whip, adorned with barbaric splendor, is handsome in a cold, brutal way. His horse is beautiful in a different sense. Here one feels Gordon's affection and admiration for a lovable being. Gordon's identification with horse and rider seem to belong to two different emotional strata. The rider seems to embody all the real and imagined dangers which threaten the little boy's manhood and very life. Gordon hides his fear and helplessness behind this ferocious mask. The horse, on the other hand, embodies the inner resources which Gordon mobilizes as he becomes one with his friend the swift and powerful horse. Yet Gordon's friend belongs to the animal world, it remains dumb and isolated and the Mexican rider dominates the picture. The painting remains primarily an expression of Gordon's defenses. It embodies the edifice of self love, cruelty, and virtuosity which Gordon has erected to ward off emotional dangers from without and within. The painting constitutes an act of sublimation in a limited sense only. Gordon has created a beautiful form for the expression of his defenses, but since his deeper emotions are barely touched, the beauty of his painting remains cold and barren.

Our presentation of Gordon's artistic development ends at this point. With the painting of the Spanish dancer Gordon reached the consummation and end of a period. His later painting belongs to a development stage which could not unfold in school which was geared to the needs of 8 to 12 year old children.

With 13 years of age Gordon was definitely ready to leave Wiltwyck. He had accepted the idea of living for a while in the agency's residential home in the City, which was supposed to open within a few months. Within the limitations of his disturbance Gordon was ready to make every effort to adjust to a new situation.

Just at this time the agency's plans for the residential home were delayed for an indefinite time. Gordon had to spend another year at Wiltwyck without definite plans for the future. The year was marked by stagnation in all areas. Gordon virtually ceased painting. Since he was thoroughly bored and disgusted with an environment which had become stale and empty after 4 years, he no longer sketched. His perfectionism increased. He could complete nothing since he would tolerate no mistakes. Gordon's inhibition was aggravated by his father's attitude. Mr. A. was himself a frustrated painter and a perfectionist. He alternated between dreams of fame and success for the son and severe unjust criticism. Both parents were disappointed in Gordon's academic retardation and tried to focus their hopes on his artistic ability with the result of a severe blocking in both fields. Gordon's progress in reading was minimal and his paintings remained fragments.

It is interesting that the only completed paintings of the year were a car with a robber who is picking up a wad of money, a beautiful new Cadillac on display, and a golden coach with driver and servant in old fashioned Spanish clothes. In other words, Gordon's mind was focussed entirely on the acquisition of wealth and on departure.

As the school year drew to a close, it was evident that another year at Wiltwyck would be disastrous for Gordon. Yet it was not possible to find placement in another institution for the child. There was no alternative than to discharge Gordon to his parent's care. Because of his academic retardation and special talents a schedule was arranged with Gordon's new school which provided maximum time for art and shop work. Remedial reading and case work continued. After nearly 3 months Gordon seemed to have made a good initial adjustment. At the time of the writing of this case history, too short a time has elapsed for making predictions about Gordon's further fate at home and in the community.

Discussion

If we were to look at the five paintings of Gordon's which are reproduced in this study, forgetting for the moment all we know about the boy, we would see before all the work of a gifted, precocious child artist with a passionate and romantic disposition. His first beginnings are not particularly impressive. His Eskimo (Fig. 22) and his two swordfighters (Fig. 23) could have been painted by any talented boy of 9 or 10 years of age. The Egyptian princess (Fig. 24), the white whale (Fig. 25), the pencil sketches (Fig. 26), and finally the Spanish dancer, at 13 years of age (Plate VIII colorprint) are far above the average. Those paintings would be exceptional among children of any social stratum or intellectual endowment.

The paintings indicate certain problems and disturbances. They show fantasies of a phallic mother, anxieties and castration fears, and fascination with woman. There are indications of strong narcissism and bisexuality which are to be expected in an artistic personality. Yet there is nothing which indicates that the painter of those pictures has a severe learning inhibition and is virtually incapable of relationships. Gordon's paintings show no intellectual retardation. His emotional development seems as a whole to follow a normal pattern. His animals and people have no bizarre features. His power of observation and orientation seem astute and undisturbed. His earliest self-representation as an Eskimo shows Gordon lonesome and immobile but complete. The battle in front of the castle expresses normal Oedipal fantasies and healthy self-assertion.

On the basis of his earliest paintings (Figs. 22 and 23) we would rather be inclined to admire the inner strength of a little boy who produces such well-integrated paintings at a time when he has been cast out into a strange environment, without means of communication with mother and siblings, without definite knowledge even of their whereabouts and fate. We can sympathize with Gordon's inability to relate to people and understand his unwillingness to learn. Gordon is waiting for the mother's return and this waiting absorbs his emotional faculties completely. Action is suspended and Gordon seems frozen in a state of expectancy wherein the present and the world around him have lost their meaning.

Gordon's withdrawal becomes a matter of serious concern only when it continues past the usual period of grief and Gordon's emotional life seems permanently limited to a strong narcissism and a longing for mother and siblings, so that all development which necessitates the forming of new relationships is inhibited.

Speculations on the cause of this emotional deadlock remain conjectures. We know both from Gordon's paintings and from the observations of the social worker that Gordon's mother was at once an alluring and fascinating woman and an elusive, unmotherly person. Her precarious mental health created a feeling of danger and impending doom about her person. Her strong attachment to Gordon lacked motherly affection. Continuous tension of seduction, partial satisfaction and frustration, may have brought about Gordon's obsessive absorption in the relationship. We recall that living with the mother created unbearable tensions in the 8 year old and that Gordon had acted like a desperate person before admission to Wiltwyck. His destructive and self-destructive behavior lessened upon separation from her. The disappearance of Gordon's delinquent tendencies and establishment of inner controls seems one of the important gains at Wiltwyck.

The reasons for the severity of Gordon's reading block remain obscure. His denial of the reality of his family situation and his fantasizing may have made him fearful of the exactitude and discipline of the written word. His mother's intellectual demands, her own love of books, may have aroused Gordon's obstinancy. His later inability to overcome his inhibitions even to the point of acquiring the rudiments of reading seem linked to his inability to form relationships to a teacher.

Gordon's chief means of communication is his art. Here Gordon is able to give expression to his innermost feelings, and as times goes on his language becomes increasingly refined and articulate. At 13 years of age Gordon is developing many of the characteristics of the dedicated artist. He concentrates his abilities in his chosen field, emulates the past and present master painters of the school, and is determined to surpass them all. He takes a benevolent interest in younger, talented children and tells them of his early beginnings. He often promises to a child that he will become just as good a painter as he himself if he stays at the school and continues to come to art sessions. He identifies with the art therapist's profession and teaching methods and needs her approval. His lasting and intense identification with the art of Wiltwyck, with the school's past and present artists and the art therapist seem a substitute for his missing personal relationships.

A development of this kind would be impossible without a strong innate talent. Yet talent alone does not make an artist. Only an overpowering need for communication through the particular medium of form and color mobilizes the intensity and singleminded concentration which distinguishes the dedicated artist from the gifted amateur. In Gordon's case it may well have been the very lack of other avenues of communication which brought about a blossoming in the field of art. His narcissism, his need to fantasize and his isolation may have forced the choice of a medium wherein creation remains a solitary experience, independent of a group.

In view of his deficiences it seems probable that Gordon's painting helped to prevent a more serious crippling of his personality. As Gordon grows older, his painting becomes closer linked to his reality situation. Between 13 and 14 Gordon experiences a total disillusionment in his parents. When the agency is unable to offer definite plans for his future Gordon's productive powers break down under the weight of his helplessness and disappointment. He retires into compulsive, meticulous kinds of work, and becomes unable to complete his pictures. The return of his productivity would depend on a change of his reality situation.

It would be futile at this point to attempt a prognosis of Gordon's future fate as artist and as a human being. There is no way of foreseeing whether his precarious mental balance will withstand the storms of adolescence, or whether his dedication to art will continue into adulthood. Much depends on the reality situation of the next years. Gordon's talent, his personality, and his childhood experiences seem to forecast the persistence of his artistic aspirations. His deep disturbance, academic retardation, and the need to earn a living make a future as a painter questionable.

Gordon's art at 13 years of age shows his deficiencies as a human being. Gordon is not a sympathetic painter. His work, though admirable, lacks directness. An uneasy romanticism and cold virtuosity give proof of his sexual confusion and emotional withdrawal. The later development of Gordon's style cannot be deduced from his adolescent painting.

Gordon's history has led beyond the scope of this study. We have touched upon the mystery of the structure and development of the artistic personality. Our description ends at a point where Gordon's ultimate fate as an artist and human being is still uncertain. Gordon's history shows the possibilities and limitations of art therapy with particular clarity. Therapeutic insight and the serious teaching of art become closely linked whenever it is the art therapist's good fortune to help a gifted disturbed child to preserve and develop his talent and draw sustenance from it in his struggle for rehabilitation.

BIBLIOGRAPHY

ALPERT, A.: Observations on the treatment of emotionally disturbed children in a therapeutic center. *Psychoanalyt. Stud. Child, 9:*334, 1954.

AICHORN, A.: *Wayward Youth.* New York, Viking, 1935.

ALSHULER, R., and HATTWICK, B. W.: *Painting and Personality.* Chicago, Univ. Chicago Press, 1947.

BENDER, L.: Art and therapy in the mental disturbance of children. *J. Nerv. & Ment. Dis., 86:*249, 1937.

BENEDICT, R.: *Patterns of Culture,* New York, Mentor Books, New American Library, 1950.

BERNFELD, S.: Bemerkungen über Sublimierung. *Imago, 8:* 333, 1922.

BERNFELD, S.: Zur Sublimierungstheorie. *Imago, 17:*339, 1931.

BETTELHEIM, B.: *Love is Not Enough.* Glencoe, Illinois, Free Press, 1950.

BETTELHEIM, B.: *Truants from Life.* Glencoe, Illinois, Free Press, 1955.

BETTELHEIM, B.: *Symbolic Wounds.* Glencoe, Illinois, Free Press, 1954.

BORNSTEIN, B.: On latency. *Psychoanalyt. Stud. Child, 6:*65, 1951.

CROCKER, D.: Study of a problem of aggression. *Psychoanalyt. Stud. Child, 10:*300, 1955.

DUBOIS, C.: *The People of Alor.* Minnesota, Univ. Minnesota Press, 1944.

EISSLER, R.: Scapegoats of society, in *Searchlights on Delinquency,* K. R. Eissler, editor. New York, Internat. Univ. Press, 1949.

FAURE, E.: *L'Esprit de Formes.* Paris, Georges Cres & Cie, 1922.

FREUD, A.: *The Ego and the Mechanisms of Defense.* New York, Internat. Univ. Press, 1946.

FREUD, A.: Aggression in relation to emotional development normal and pathological. *Psychoanalyt. Stud. Child, 314*:37, 1949.

FREUD, A.: The mutual influences in the development of ego and id. *Psychoanalyt. Stud. Clin.* 7:42, 1952.

FREUD, A.: Certain types and stages of a social maladjustment, in *Searchlights on Delinquency,* K. R. Eissler, editor. New York, Internat. Univ. Press, 1949.

FREUD, A., and BURLINGHAM, D. T.: *Infants Without Families.* New York, Internat. Univ. Press, 1944.

FREUD, A., and BURLINGHAM, D. T.: *War and Children.* New York Internat. Univ. Press, 1943.

FREUD, A., and BURLINGHAM, D. T.: *Young Children in War Time.* London, Allen & Unwin, 1942.

FREUD, S.: *Leonardo da Vinci.* New York, Dodd, 1932.

FREUD, S.: The Moses of Michaelangelo (1914) in Complete Psychological Works of Freud, Vol. 13. London, Hogarth Press, 1955.

FREUD, S.: The interpretation of dreams (1900), in *The Basic Writings of Sigmund Freud.* New York, Modern Library, 1938.

FREUD, S.: Three contributions to the theory of sex (1905), in *The Basic Writings of Sigmund Freund.* New York, Modern Library, 1938.

FREUD, S.: Instincts and their vicissitudes (1915), in *Collected Papers,* Vol. 4. London, Hogarth Press, 1925.

FREUD, S.: The infantile genital organization and the libido (1925), in *Collected Papers,* Vol. 2. London, Hogarth Press, 1924.

FREUD, S.: On the sexual theories of children (1908), in *Collected Papers,* Vol. 2. London, Hogarth Press, 1924.

FREUD, S.: Formulations regarding the two principles of mental functioning (1911), in *Collected Papers,* Vol. 4. London, Hogarth Press, 1925.

FREUD, S.: Character and anal eroticism (1908), in *Collected Papers*, Vol. 2. London, Hogarth Press, 1924.
FREUD, S.: The unconscious (1915), in *Collected Papers*, Vol. 4. London, Hogarth Press, 1925.
FREUD, S.: The passing of the oedipus complex (1942), in *Collected Papers*, Vol. 4. London, Hogarth Press, 1925.
FREUD, S.: The relation of the poet to daydreaming (1908), in *Collected Works*, Vol. 2. London, Hogarth Press, 1924.
FREUD, S.: The uncanny (1919), in *Standard Edition*, Vol. 17. London, Hogarth Press, 1955.
FREUD, S.: *The Ego and the Id*. London, Hogarth Press, 1927.
FREUD, S.: A neurosis of demoniacal possession in the Seventeenth Century (1923), in *Collected Papers*, Vol. 4. London, Hogarth Press, 1925.
FREUD, S.: *Group Psychology and the Analysis of the Ego*. New York, Liveright, 1940.
FREUD, S.: *The Problem of Anxiety*. New York, Norton, 1936.
FREUD, S.: *Inhibition Symptom and Anxiety*. London, Hogarth Press, 1936.
FRAIBERG, S.: Enlightenment and confusion. *Psychoanalyl. Stud. Child*, *6*:325, 1951.
GREENACRE, P.: Swift and Carroll. New York, Internat. Univ. Press, 1955.
HARTMAN, H.: Notes on the theory of sublimation. *Psychoanalyt. Stud. Child*. *10*:9, 1955.
HELLERSBERG, E.: *The Individual's Relationship to Reality in our Culture*. Springfield, Thomas, 1950.
JONES, E.: *Hamlet and Oedipus*. London, S. Gollancz, 1949.
KRIS, E.: *Psychoanalytic Explorations in Art*. New York, Internat. Univ. Press, 1952.
KRIS, E.: Neutralization and sublimation: Observations on young children. *Psychoanalyt. Stud. Child*. *10*:30, 1955.
KRIS, E.: On psychoanalysis and education. *Am. J. Orthopsychiat.*, *18*:622, 1948.

LEE, H. B.: The values of order and vitality in art, in *Psychoanalysis and Social Sciences*, G. Roheim, editor. New York, Internat. Univ. Press, 1950, pp. 231-274.

LEE, H. B.: *The Beautiful.* London, Cambridge Univ. Press, 1913.

LISS, E.: The graphic arts. *Am. J. Orthopsychiatry*, 8:95, 1938.

LOWENFELD, H.: Psychic trauma and productive experience in the artist. *Psychoanalyst. Quart.*, 10:116, 1941.

MACHOVER, K.: *Personality Projection in the Drawing of the Human Figure.* Springfield, Thomas, 1952.

McCORD, W., and McCORD, J.: *Psychopathy and Delinquency.* New York, Grune & Stratton, 1956.

MUMFORD, L.: Irritional elements in art and politics, in *In the Name of Sanity.* New York, Harcourt, 1954.

MUMFORD, L.: *Art and Technics.* New York, Harcourt, 1934.

MUNZ, L., and LOEWENFELD, V.: *Plastische Arbeiten Blinder.* Brunn, Rudolf M. Rohrer, 1934.

NAUMBURG, M.: *Studies of the "Free" Art Expression of Behavior Problem Children and Adolescents as a Means of Diagnosis and Therapy.* New York, Nerv. and Ment. Dis. Monographs, 1947.

NAUMBURG, M.: *Psychoneurotic Art, It's Function in Psychotherapy.* New York, Grune & Stratton, 1950.

OBERHOLZER, E.: Rorschach's experiment and the Alorese, in *The People of Alor*, by C. Dubois. Minneapolis, Univ. Minnesota Press, 1944.

OBERNDORF, C. P.: Psychotherapy in a resident children's group, in *Searchlight on Delinquency*, K. R. Eissler, editor. New York, Internat. Univ. Press, 1949.

OLDEN, C.: About the fascinating effect of the narcissistic personality. *American Imago*, 2:347, 1941.

OLDEN, C.: On adult empathy with children. *Psychoanalyt. Stud. Child.* 8:111, 1953.

RANK, O.: *Art and Artist.* New York, Knopf, 1932.

REDL, F.: Contagion and shock effect, in *Searchlights on Delinquency*. K. R. Eissler, editor. New York, Internat. Univ. Press, 1949.

REDL, F., and WINEMANN, D.: *Children Who Hate*. Glencoe, Illinois, Free Press, 1951.

REDL, F., and WINEMAN, D.: *Controls from Within*. Glencoe, Illinois, Free Press, 1952.

REICH, A.: Structure of the grotesque-comic sublimation. *Bull. Menninger Clin., 13:*160, 171, 1949.

REVESZ, G.: *Talent und Genie*. Bern, A. Francke Verlag, 1952.

ROHEIM, H.: Sublimation. *Psychoanalyt. Quart., 12:*338, 1943.

RORSCHACH, H.: *Psychodiagnostics*. New York, Grune & Stratton, 1927.

SACHS, H.: *The Creative Unconscious*. Cambridge, Massachusetts, Sci-Art Publishers, 1942.

SCHMIDL-WAEHNER, T.: Formal Criteria for the Analysis of Children's Drawings. *Am. J. Orthopsychiat., 12:*95, 1942.

INDEX

A

A., Mrs., 194-197, 205, 212, 214, 215
Adams, Charles, 101
Adolescence, 31, 225
Advisory board, professional, 32
Albert, 149-152
Altdorfer, Albrecht, 86
Aggression, 12, 54, 102, 107, 143, 148; *See also* Hostility
  anal, 43, 154
  and art therapy, 141-172
  behavior, 141-143, 157
  binding of, 147, 149
  cannibalistic, 99
  channeling of, 144, 145
  as emotional content in art, 146
  devouring, 103, 156, 157, 203
  neutralization, 53
  transformation of, 143, 144, 152
Ambivalence, 35, 38, 123, 181, 187, 190, 199
Andersen, Hans Christian, 89, 163
Anxiety, *See also* Fear
  absence of, 83
  in art, 47, 133
  binding of, 168
  castration, 153
  mastery of, 97
  neutralized, 53
  outward directed, 97
  victory over, 178
Art
  adolescent, 226
  adult, 19, 102
  bizarre, 43, 52-60, 81-108
  and childhood, 18-20
  communication in, 7-11, 15, 224
  decorative, 103, 104
  and form, 9
  and hypocrisy, 10, 172
  material, 36, 37
  perfectionism in, 190
  primitive, 47, 102
  and reality, 8
  social function of, 40, 41
  and society, 7-11
  teaching, 224
  unconscious content in, 8
Art teacher
  and art therapist, 22
Art therapist
  communication with student, 5
  and community, 35
  as controlling influence, 141-143
  cooperation with psychotherapist, 108
  as educator, 125-140
  function, 5-7, 51, 52, 107, 170
  identification with, 212, 224
  and individual therapy, 35
  intervention, 108, 177, 185
  participation, 135
  relationship to, 217, 218
  role of, 21, 23, 42, 43
  testing of, 181, 182
Art therapy
  and art, 7
  and audience, 21-23
  beyond reach of, 171
  communication in, 21-23
  definition, 5-7
  and diagnosis, 5
  and group situation, 41
  and integration, 21
  program, 21-23, 35-41
  termination of, 23

Index

Art therapy sessions
  attendance, 94, 127
  behavior in, 185
  mood during, 176, 178
  termination of, 166
Artist
  adolescent, 216
  adult, 19, 215
  and audience, 9-11, 59, 60
  character structure, 19, 143, 144, 170
  child, 222
  dedicated, 224, 225
  intuition, 16, 17
  and narcissism, 16
  personality, 11, 17, 18, 51, 225
  and voyeurism, 12, 13
Audience, response of, 8, 20, 39, 40, 41, 162, 168

B

Bernard, 79, 81
Bisexuality, 222
Board of Education, 34
Body image, 119, 120, 137

C

Carl, 66-71, 123
Carol, 194
Carroll, Lewis, 106
Castration fear, 148, 153, 156, 208, 222
Children's courts, 27
Clyde, 47-50, 83-87, 102, 104
Coeducation, 28
Communication
  and cultural tradition, 60-65
  and structure, 51, 52
Contagion in group activities, 59
Cottage parent, 32
Counselor, 32, 33
  head, 32, 33, 43, 151, 180, 190
  senior, 32
Cultural background, 49, 50

D

Daydream, 87, 101, 126
  and art, 8, 9
  grandiose, 205
  ready made, 110
Defense, 8, 152
Delinquency, 224
Delinquent
  acts, 77, 204
  adult, 28
  child, 73, 106
  environment, 73
  father, 27
Denial
  of hostility, 148, 149
  of reality, 123, 224
Department of Welfare, 27
Depersonalization, 79, 81
Depression, 67, 69, 77, 80, 98, 151, 168, 170
Director
  assistant, 32
  executive, 32
  resident, 32, 219
  of social services, 32

E

Edgar, 93, 99-102, 104
Edward, 194, 196
Ego
  conflict with id, 170
  conflict with superego, 170
  control, 103
  development, 18
  formation, 13, 103
  function, 12, 14, 58-60
  ideal, 119, 164
  impoverishment, 152
  incomplete organization, 54
  mature, 187
  strength, 17, 18, 148, 152
  unconscious area of, 22, 23
Elation, 168, 171

Empathy, 51, 79
Escape
 from hostility, 148, 199
 from reality, 119
Exhibitionism
 channeling of, 48
 gratification of, 49, 50
Exhibition
 of children's paintings, 35
 therapeutic function of, 40, 41, 43-50

F

Frustration
 tolerance, 130
 threshold, 143
Frank, 175-194
Folder, therapeutic value of, 138-140, 184
Flecher, 124
Fixation
 anal, 148
 oral, 148
Fantasies
 aggressive, 162
 and art, 8, 9
 of birth, 109
 bizarre, 106
 of future, 212
 fusion with reality, 123
 grandiose, 213
 masochistic, 104
 masturbatory, 104
 oedipal, 223
 of phallic mother, 222
 preoccupation with, 126
 reassuring, 154
 sexual, 210, 211
Finger paint, 36, 37

G

Gordon, 194-226
Gratification
 instinctual, 142, 163
 narcissistic, 72, 167, 168, 205

Group
 behavior, 69
 ideal, 73
 and individual, 41-43
 pressure, 190
 therapist, 33
Guilt, 84, 85, 101, 123, 163, 164
 absence of, 83
 for aggressive fantasies, 104, 105

H

Hals, Frans, 73
Harry, 87-94, 101, 104
Hostility, 176; *See* Aggression
 to mother, 180, 181

I

Id, 14
Identification
 with aggressor, 147, 153-155, 167
 with art therapist, 39-41
 with father, 181
 within the group, 39-41
 with hero, 154
 process of, 120
 with teacher, 128
Identity, feeling of, 120, 122
Imitation, 120
Impulse
 aggressive, 6, 17, 163
 asocial, 11
 control, 30, 80, 150, 163
 destructive, 147, 169
 gratification, 162
 libidinal, 17
 mastery, 18
 overwhelming, 104
 power of, 148
Incorporation
 of objects, 17
 of style elements, 58
Inhibitions, 224
 loss of, 171

Instinct
  control, 12
  gratification, 12
Integration
  in art, 100, 187
  into community, 45
Internalization
  of conflict, 159
  of feelings, 77
Interpretation
  of unconscious content, 5

J

Jacky, 130-132, 136
Jerry, 71-76, 79, 80, 83
John, 52-60

K

Klee, Paul, 53, 106

L

Latency, 182
  and art, 18
Learning
  disturbance, 204
  process of, 125-140

M

Martin, 35, 36, 49, 50, 53, 60-65, 66-71, 109
Marvin, 155-159
Masochism, 145, 146
Matthew, 93-98, 101, 104, 108, 124, 152
Moby Dick, 208-210
Monster painting, 81-108, 176
Moral code
  differences of, 63, 64
  incorporation of, 30
Moral values
  absence of, 84, 88
  establishment of, 206
  expressed in art, 203

N

Neurosis
  and sublimation, 15, 143
Neutralization
  of aggression, 16, 143
  of anxiety, 85
  and art, 16, 143
Nurse, 34, 219

O

Odysseus, 176, 177
Oedipus complex, 153

P

Paul, 52-60, 83-85, 87, 93, 104
Perception and skill, 134-136
Pre-puberty and art, 18
Primary process, 103, 105
Projection of aggression, 159-169
Psychiatrist, 33
Psychologist, 33, 189
Psychotherapist, 5, 33
Psychotherapy, 181
  use of art in, 5
  individual, 94

R

Ralph, 135, 136
Raymond, 43-46, 49, 50
Raymund, 145-148
Reaction formation, 15, 151
Reading, remedial, 34, 212, 215, 222
Reality, 109-124
Redon, Odilion, 86
Regression, 97, 142, 167, 171, 186
  controlled, 172
  and painting, 98
  and sublimation, 14
  uncontrolled, 172
Relationship, 109-124
Rembrandt, 73
Repression, 8, 16, 211
Residential home, 214, 220, 221
Resistance against learning, 127-140

Index

Retaliation, 105
Richard, 130, 132-134
Robert, 175, 176, 191
Ronny, 136

S

Seduction, 223
 and sublimation, 58, 59
Selassie, Haile, 62
Self-acceptance, 136-138, 168
Self-destruction, 139, 169-171
Self identity, 119
Self representation, 110, 121, 124, 168
Sex play, 198
Sexual curiosity, 208
Sexuality
 aggressive, 148
 degraded, 208
Social worker, 32, 94, 214, 215
 psychiatric, 33
 supervisor, 33
Style, 51, 52, 125, 188
 change of, 94, 105
 conventional, 164
 mutual influences in, 41, 42
 rise and decline of, 66
 stereotyped, 64
 and society, 9, 10
Subject matter, 109-124
Sublimation
 in art, 15-18
 of aggression, 159
 of conflict, 152, 189
 definition, 13
 deprivation of, 125, 126
 of destructive impulses, 150
 of fantasies, 58
 genuine, 7
 incomplete, 6, 159, 163
 level, 45
 process of, 169, 194
 and renunciation, 12
 successful, 164
 theory of, 11-15

Superego
 aggressive, 170
 approval, 14
 demands, 14
 development, 12, 13
 formation, 30
 sadistic, 170
 weakness, 148
Sybil, 194, 196
Symbol, 96, 98, 99, 102, 110, 120
 phallic, 123, 155, 156
 of potency, 138
 primitive, 119
Symbolism
 bizarre, 84
 private, 100
Symptom, 93, 94, 97, 145, 146

T

Talion, law of, 104
Theodore, 159-164
Therapist, dance, 34
Therapy, symbolic quality, 21
Theresa, 194
Thurber, James, 101
Tradition
 formation of, 69
 rise and fall, 70
Transference, 22
 to art therapist, 168, 179
 in art therapy, 22, 129, 130
 in psychotherapy, 22, 129
 to social worker, 129
Treatment, accessibility, 95
Treatment home, 27-35
Twin
 fraternal, 130
 relationship, 54-60, 84

U

Unconscious, 18, 101
 in art, 23

V

Van Dyke, 73

W

Walter, 75-77, 80, 102, 135-136, 164-169, 216

Wiltwyck School, 27-35, 43-45, 142, 175, 196
    children of, 52
    population, 28
    staff, 32-35
    treatment program, 32-35

Withdrawal, 226
    narcissistic, 80

Y

YMCA swimming pool, 121